The Storeroom of the Heart

JESUS' MODEL FOR AN ABUNDANT LIFE

Charles W. Short

CROSSBOOKS
PUBLISHING

CrossBooks™
A Division of LifeWay
1663 Liberty Drive
Bloomington, IN 47403
www.crossbooks.com
Phone: 1-866-879-0502

First published by CrossBooks 06/26/2012

ISBN: 978-1-4627-1946-4 (sc)
ISBN: 978-1-4627-1948-8 (hc)
ISBN: 978-1-4627-1947-1 (e)

Library of Congress Control Number: 2012910757

Printed in the United States of America

This book is printed on acid-free paper.

For every person who has been disappointed in their Christian walk, but wasn't able to define what was holding them back. May God use this work to help you become more than you are and more than you ever expected.

Contents

Guard your heart above all else,
for it is the source of life.
Proverbs 4:23

Many people have helped me understand and refine these materials over the last several years. Certain ones have been sample readers; others encouragers. All have helped me to make this material better. Jane Moses, Sara Staley, Cara Hayley, Bonnie Brewster, and Ellen Staley read the material as it took shape and gave helpful advice in its development. Alycia W. Morales took on the task of helping with final edits. My sweet wife, Stephanie, put up with my moodiness as I wrestled with both the content and the sense of calling that mandated I seek its publication.

Chapter 1

The football quake

In 2004, my son started high school football. His freshman year, a new coach arrived. A new coach meant a new program, new plays, new plans, and new attitudes. Change washed over the team and offered them better opportunities.

The school tolerated a lackluster football program for years. This community and its families expected little of their kids in general and devalued high school sports. Accordingly, the team never expected success, and their record reflected their attitude.

I had the privilege of listening in on some of the speeches the coach gave the players. The coach had a habit of reiterating the boys must play with heart. I heard those words of encouragement, but the significance of the word *heart* eluded me.

During this time, an imperceptible struggle took place among the players. Each player made an internal decision about themselves, determining how much effort they wanted to put into their football skills and developing their own character.

Every year their season began with a game between their school and another local high school. This game was a grudge match for my son's school, but not a very fair one. The other school was a larger school, playing in a higher division. Having a bigger school meant more players on the team and opportunities to pick better, stronger players. This school emphasized football. Consequently, every year, the competing school won.

They began their conference games with an attitude of victory, while my son's school started the season with a bitter defeat.

The crowd expected nothing different at the start of the game that year. Tradition required the teams play, but everyone anticipated the smaller school would be thoroughly whipped and sent home with their tail between their legs. For the first half of the game, it appeared no patterns would be broken. The large school scored with relative ease and at the half enjoyed a comfortable lead. Meanwhile, the players for the smaller school seemed unprepared and unfocused. They didn't line up straight. They didn't come onto the field together. Worst of all, they squabbled among themselves.

After the half, I watched with interest as the team came back out on the field. Was it my imagination, or did they run differently and stand taller? The special teams lined up for the kickoff at the start of the third quarter. I noticed small, significant improvements in behavior. For example, the entire group came out together instead of straggling out in disarray. They found their positions precisely instead of haphazardly. These adjustments were minor. What caught my eye, excited the crowd, and demonstrated something had changed came next. In perfect unison, every player on the line dropped into a four-point stance.

Is a four-point stance overkill for a kickoff? (Well, yeah. But if we are determined to break a pattern, go for overkill.) What does it take to have a previously disjointed team all move in one synchronized, fluid movement? What inside the heart of these football players changed so dramatically their efforts went from unfocused to choreographed? The kicker's foot found the ball, and every player launched into a spring-loaded charge at an unsuspecting team of opponents.

The second half of the game bore no resemblance to the first. The crowd knew it, the opposing team knew it, and, most important, the underdogs knew it. The pattern was about to be broken, even shattered. The crowd sensed the change and roared its approval. The underdogs scored repeatedly. The local world of football shifted with the power of a minor earthquake. And in the aftershocks, several high school football players learned they were capable of more than they considered possible.

The smaller school won the game, but it didn't matter. The important issue for the moment was not the victory, but replacing the pattern. Because they won the internal battle, the external game followed. From that game forward, they were a changed team. For the first time in years, they qualified in their division and went to state. They went to state the next year, too. For as long as the new coach remained at their school, they won.

At the end of the game, the stands emptied onto the field. Players, coaches, spectators, and other parents enjoyed the adrenaline high provided by the accomplishment. In the mad rush of those moments, I congratulated the coach and commented, "The second half was played with remarkable heart."

The coach looked straight at me and said, "This team is all about heart."

The words were brief, but they had a larger-than-life impact on me. Long after the encounter, I kept thinking about those words. What did he mean the team was all about heart?

Although I heard him, and many others, use the term heart, I wasn't sure what each person meant by it. After several days of my mind returning to the idea, I began to look into the concept of heart. It became a journey of surprising simplicity, a series of somewhat obvious conclusions. However, I have learned, people forget obvious things as easily as they forget more complicated matters.

I came to ask serious questions of this attribute we call heart. What exactly is heart? How can it be intelligibly defined? Is it something we are either born with or without? If we are not born with it, are we able to learn it, teach it, and choose to apply it? If heart is an attribute that fuels achievement in our lives, then can we channel the power of heart at will into different areas of life?

I found the answers to these questions in the Bible. Heart can be learned and intentionally applied. Its characteristics can be understood and controlled for the glory of God. It's actually pretty simple. Not easy, but simple. In the long run, the most important question will not be can we control heart, but will we? If we accept the scriptural model of heart, God will bless us with greater accomplishments and a higher sense of purpose.

Everyone desires success. We don't all go about it the same way, but we want to accomplish something significant. We need our lives to matter. We have an innate desire to make a difference, and for those who know Jesus Christ as Savior, we long to make an eternal difference.

A sense of purpose and accomplishment eludes most people. Worse yet, at some point in life the difficulties and disappointments bring us to an unholy compromise. After enough heartache, we give up on our desire to excel. We no longer endeavor to do our best, not even our best for God. We don't mind if our achievements don't add up to so much, as long as they don't come down to too little. It's a very pragmatic compromise. When it becomes apparent we aren't going to soar with the eagles, we stop focusing on the heights above and, instead, watch the depths below. Rather than striving to see how high we can reach, our focus shifts to avoid sinking too low. Somewhere in the process we lose heart.

Is it necessary? Is it a part of growing up and taking on the responsibilities of maturity? Is it a shift everyone must go through? Is it the idealism of youth passing away? If you feel skeptical about these assertions, then you are like me. I am not convinced we live the life we are meant to live. This compromise more closely resembles a plan of Satan's than a desire of God's. Unfortunately, most people have embraced this concession.

Christians look like the rest of the world. My Bible says we are to be different. But divorce rates, addiction rates, and bankruptcy rates of those professing Christ are roughly equal with those not professing Christ. I am not aware of any statistic indicating Christians are living differently than the rest of the world. This is not how it ought to be.

I believe somewhere deep in my core, God made us–and especially remade us in Christ–to live our lives as a wonderful adventure. When He called us into His family, through the redemption of Jesus Christ, His intention was to re-create us to live a life that rose above the mediocrity around us. "Mount up on wings of eagles," the Bible says. But is this the experience we are living? The Christian life I have lived in the past is not entirely the one intended for me.

Before I go on, let me make sure we do not misunderstand. I am not implying we are not saved. I am not criticizing the church or the way it functions. I also am not stating Christianity is ineffective. But I *am* saying we could be better: more effective as God's army on earth, more able to make an eternal difference. We could, and in fact should, rise higher than we have.

I believe some people live above this compromise. These people are over comers. They are available for and achieve God's purposes in their lives. I do not suppose these men and women of accomplishment are "charmed," making their success easier. Rather, I believe they live out some simple principles that unlock opportunities most of us miss. I think those principles can be learned and applied to give us all potential to be one of those conquerors who live and accomplish with heart.

My maternal grandfather suffered for years with colon cancer but refused to die. Not because of a fear of death or a love of life. He refused to die because he had made a commitment to his wife. My grandmother had Alzheimer's. He believed her care was his responsibility. Rather than succumb to the pain and to the disease, he fought off the inevitable until after his wife went home to be with Jesus. Then, and only then, he let the Lord know he was ready. A mere twenty days later he also went home, having lived out his commitment. Where does the power to resist cancer come from? This is the power of heart.

There are scriptural principles to enable us to live above normal circumstances. We will benefit from learning these practices, but in order to understand them fully, we need to first lay a foundation.

Chapter 2

Careless colloquialism

I am well aware of the ambiguity that exists in definition. Do you remember being in the fifth grade and the teacher giving a writing assignment to complete the sentence, "Love is . . . ?" Teachers give this assignment because it forces their students to discuss abstract concepts. And to a fifth grader, love is very abstract.

The completed assignments contained many common themes, but in every student's mind there remained a unique concept of love. They bore similarity to one another, but subtle differences also existed, reflecting what the word meant to each individual writer. God bless anyone able to verbalize such nuances in the fifth grade.

We need to embrace a new and better understanding of the term heart. This will cause us to wade into similarly murky waters. Before asking us to settle on a definition, we should wrestle with what the word means to us now. Hopefully this process will help us to stop using the word ambiguously. When I divulge my functional definition, I want us to be prepared for the term to have a concrete meaning.

The term has several predominant usages, and perhaps when the coach used it he meant one of these or some combination of them. Let me step through a few of these different definitions, attempting to find some key ingredients to what different individuals mean when they speak of heart.

Five ingredients are often used to make up the definition of heart:

1. There are emotional aspects of the word.
2. The word reflects the amount of effort one is willing to give.

3. Heart defines one's self-esteem or confidence.
4. It encompasses one's core values.
5. The term describes a person's courage.

When I started looking into these ideas, it was easiest for me to consider heart as an issue of the emotions. Heart describes what we love, what we care about, what arouses our passions in such a way as to prompt us to action. When we say something "tugs at our heart strings," we mean it affects us emotionally. When we proclaim we love someone, we consider it a deeper expression to love them "with all our heart." In these and a multitude of other ways, we use the term heart to refer to our emotional state or for the basis of feelings, but heart must involve more than an emotional dynamic. I have heard athletes say they won because they wanted it more than the other team. But the desire was useless unless it resulted in a lot of disciplined practice, teamwork, an understanding of the game, and the courage to risk for the sake of the prize.

The second ingredient often used to define a person who performs with heart is determination, how hard they are able and willing to work. I assumed the coach meant this when he told me his team was all about heart. I originally thought he spoke of how hard they fought the battle on the gridiron that day. Every year some of the young men pushed themselves to physical exhaustion, while others only pushed when the coach was watching. Others didn't seem to care even when the coach stood over them. We all recognize those with the best work ethic express the greatest heart. Heart has to be more than determination, because great effort can be exerted in all the wrong directions. In order for effort to be heart, it must be focused on the right activities.

A third common facet of the term is a person's belief in him- or herself. Some readily assume they can accomplish anything they sincerely attempt. Others maintain a less complimentary self-image and highlight their faults and short-comings. The first of these two reflects a person with more heart, and the latter reflects a person whose heart has been injured in some manner. This illustrates the manner in which self-confidence is a part of what we mean when we say a person has heart. But one's esteem without any of these other virtues becomes an over-inflated ego, a matter of pride, so this self-assurance cannot stand alone to define heart.

A fourth potential way of looking at heart is how a person's core values make up their heart. If a person values helping others and works consistently for the public good, then we consider them to be a person of heart. If their value system is selfish and considers only their own good, we consider them to be heartless. Therefore, well-placed and selfless moral foundations are another component of heart. Core values are useless until those values result in appropriate action. A solid definition of right and wrong falls short unless we also shape our behavior to match the values.

A final ingredient in how heart is defined by public usage is the practice of courage. When a person loses their courage, we say they "lose heart." In Scripture it sometimes says a person's "heart melted," referring to their becoming afraid. In the same way, a person who stands their ground or moves ahead with courage is "strong hearted." Courage alone is not a complete understanding of what heart is and means. One can go bravely about doing heartless activities, so it is not enough to have courage. One must also employ their courage in worthy tasks.

We have examined five different ingredients we can combine in any number of ways to produce a definition of heart. We have also pointed out weaknesses in all of these elements. Notice how some of the components overlap each other. This, too, is a part of the ambiguity of language.

For example, determination relates to emotions since the hard work only takes place when it is driven by a desire. This desire is a matter of emotion. How hard a person works also ties closely to their belief in themselves. After all, people do not work toward a goal if they believe it is beyond their ability. Our ethical base and our courage are closely related; it requires guts to live up to what we believe is right and wrong. In a few short statements we've mentioned several ways the concepts overlap.

What we have said so far is heart can be defined in a multitude of ways. Every person has a slightly different way of looking at the concept, but generally those definitions contain some mixture of one or more of these attributes: emotion, effort, confidence, morality, and courage.

If my assertion is right, heart is a powerful tool for accomplishing meaningful things in this world. The only way to unleash its potential is by having a common definition we can clearly understand and apply. Everything said about heart thus far might be true, but it's too complex to be useful in daily life.

For the remainder of this text, we'll define heart as a storeroom. It is the place inside of us where everything we think, do, and encounter is stored up. This storeroom of the heart holds on to all of these things as resources for future opportunities. A person with their heart filled well will draw out of their storeroom the resources needed for accomplishment and success. The person who stores up garbage in their hearts will be unknowingly contaminating their own potential and sabotaging their own success.

Chapter 3

God's designated storeroom

My father was a mechanic who possessed remarkable skill with engines. He worked to instill those abilities into my brothers and me. Since both of my brothers do very well with mechanical things, he succeeded. Both of them can repair their own cars, if they choose to do so. As for me, I am not quite as mechanically inclined.

But with age comes wisdom, and I have a handle on why I never conquered those skills. I got frustrated when I couldn't find a tool or a part, especially when I had it in my hand a few minutes earlier. This frustration defeated me.

One trait good mechanics share is they always put their tools away in an orderly manner. The importance of easily accessing the needed tool explains why many mechanics consider the oversized tool box their most important tool. The simple reality is you cannot get a tool from the box if you did not put it back the last time you used it.

It's obvious. You cannot take out what you did not put in. This fact about all storage containers carries over to the heart. Jesus teaches us this lesson in Matthew 12:34-35. "For the mouth speaks from the overflow of the heart. A good man produces good things from his storeroom of good, and an evil man produces evil things from his storeroom of evil."

In verse thirty-four, He says the mouth speaks what overflows from the heart, but in the next verse, He furthers the idea by stating the evil or good in a man's storeroom controls whether it is evil or good that comes out of him. Whether he is an evil or a good man innately ties to what is stored in his heart by previous activity. The definition of the heart as a storeroom is drawn directly from this teaching of Jesus.

Matthew 6:19-21 says, "Don't collect for yourselves treasures on earth, where moth and rust destroy and where thieves break in and steal. But collect for yourselves treasures in heaven, where neither moth nor rust destroys, and where thieves don't break in and steal. For where your treasure is, there your heart will be also." The last sentence in this passage teaches us the heart follows the patterns we build into our lives. Specifically, it teaches if we focus on the issues of this world, our heart will reflect this world, but if we allow our priority to be the eternal, our heart will follow suit.

Our choices fill our hearts. Like any storeroom, we can only pull out of our heart what has previously been stored in it. This is the manner in which we control what we place in our hearts, until eventually what we put in our hearts controls us. This is an important part of what Jesus said in Matthew 12:34-35, but it is understood more clearly when placed alongside Matthew 6:20-21.

Proverbs 4:23-27 is another key passage when considering the biblical use of the word heart. I find this passage intriguing when it says to guard the heart because it is the source of life. The phrase source of life means the life we have flows from our heart. It goes on from there to give specific examples of how to guard our hearts.

"Guard your heart above all else,
for it is the source of life.
Don't let your mouth speak dishonestly,
and don't let your lips talk deviously.
Let your eyes look forward;
fix your gaze straight ahead.
Carefully consider the path for your feet,
and all your ways will be established.
Don't turn to the right or to the left;
keep your feet away from evil."

What the above passage gives as instruction in how to guard our hearts is to guard our behavior, to always act with integrity. We protect our hearts by doing what is right. Since everything we are exposed to is stored in our hearts, protecting our hearts means guarding ourselves from evil and controlling what we expose ourselves to.

These passages require us to use a different definition of heart than we have used in the past. I personally had been stuck on the idea of the heart as the seat of human emotions when I saw it in Scripture. While this use may be found in a few passages, the vast majority of Scripture does not use the term in this way. The scholarly way of looking at heart has nothing to do with emotions. Scholars define the term heart as being the center or essence of a person or idea, the core principle guiding how someone or something operates.[1] This is in agreement with our functional definition, especially in teaching that the content of the heart guides a person's life.

Our definition is more useful, though, because it includes the important extra detail. Not only does the heart shape our future, but the heart itself was shaped by the past. This principle is an important part of the definition and that which allows us to use the concept of heart to our advantage. We can choose what to store in our hearts today to control our opportunities and patterns for tomorrow.

Of course, a definition like this is not useful if it is not consistent with the other passages using the word. For this reason, we will review and gain an understanding of how the word is used in the Bible and whether or not this definition applies in the majority of the usages. If we consider the entire Bible, it is used at least 560 times. The word appears in Proverbs alone at least fifty times.

I am not giving exact numbers, because the word is so often used idiomatically. For example, in the Holman Christian Standard Bible, Proverbs 23:7 says, "for as he thinks within himself, so is he." (I used the 2003 edition, HCSB reworked this passage in 2009.) This same verse in the King James Version says, "For as he thinketh in his heart, so is he." In this passage the Hebrew word is *nephesh*, which is more commonly translated soul, rather than heart. The word heart is used as a colloquialism in the King James Version.

Consider also Proverbs 15:32 in the HCSB, "Anyone who ignores instruction despises himself, but whoever listens to correction acquires good sense." These last few words come with a footnote explaining it literally says "acquires a heart" at the end of the sentence. The intention of the verse is that the person who accepts correction acquires a good heart. Based on what we have learned, this describes a person who fills their storehouse with good things, which then empowers its owner to behave well. This is synonymous with a person who has good sense.

These examples illustrate why tracing the biblical use of the word is difficult. The word lends itself to symbolic usage in any language. Sometimes the idiom may have its root in the original language, and other times the word is used as a metaphor in the English translation. Despite these difficulties, we can see some patterns that arise in the use of the word.

One very common usage is when the word describes the courage or cowardice of specific individuals. An example would be Joshua 2:11, where Rahab is describing the fear the inhabitants of Jericho felt toward the Israelites. "When we heard this, we lost heart, and everyone's courage failed because of you, for the Lord your God is God in heaven above and on earth below." The frequency of this usage of the word heart leads to the conclusion that courage is one of the most important things we store in our hearts.

In the Beatitudes, Jesus says, "Blessed are the pure in heart, because they will see God." Using the definition of the heart as a storeroom, this would be a person who has stored up only positive attributes and experiences in their heart. This person, by allowing God to be the shaper or purifier of their heart, is the person who will see God. They will see Him both by His work in this world and by dwelling with Him in eternity. This use of the heart as a storeroom of morality is also very common in Scripture.

In Proverbs, there is another usage indicating our hearts store our self-image. Proverbs 27:19 says, "As water reflects the face, so the heart reflects the person." This verse says our hearts reflect who we truly are. This usage fits our definition of the heart as a storeroom, because we can find our identity by looking into our storeroom. This Proverb also tells us how we choose to think of ourselves, good or bad, is stored in our hearts. For a fuller picture, we might compare this verse with Proverbs 23:7 discussed above.

Using our functional definition of the heart as a storehouse transforms how we understand and interpret heart in the Bible. This new explanation is not different from the previous or the scholarly definition. A significant change from using this perspective is the clear picture—we are responsible for the content of our own hearts. We make choices in regard to what gets stored there, and those choices influence our future in greater ways than we previously realized.

---

1 W. E. Vine, *Vine's Expository Dictionary of Old and New Testament Words* (Old Tappan, NJ: Fleming H. Revell Company, 1981), p. 206

Chapter 4

The overflow of the heart

Sally struggles to get her love life under control. It started when she found her emotions entangled more easily than she wanted. These emotional connections caused her to give herself physically to men on many occasions. After some time, her behavior degenerated to the point where she would meet a new man, feel a connection, and have a one night stand, even when she knew she would never see him again. She sees this as a horrendous problem. Her mother did not raise her this way. It's not how she wants to view herself, but all her attempts to change have been ineffective. She has no idea why she can't get a handle on this and despises herself for her actions.

Sally needs to admit there are a number of other choices in her life empowering her misbehavior. Sally indulges in racy movies and sensual romance novels. She lives vicariously through those characters, and every storyline and romantic nuance is stored in her heart. Mentally she knows the stories are unrealistic. Therefore, they may not be stored in her mind, but they are stored in her heart.

In addition, she sees nothing wrong with drinking in moderation. She knows alcohol lowers her inhibitions, and her judgment is altered even when her consumption is moderate, but she still has a drink from time to time. Since she doesn't have difficulty limiting her intake, she assumes this is not a problem affecting her life. She doesn't connect the use of alcohol with her relational failures.

Sally works in an isolated office and doesn't limit the discussions which take place. Her coworkers gather there for conversations or jokes that would get them fired if spoken in the front office. She has heard an enormous amount of sensual and sexual discussion, all of which were stored up in her heart. This is every bit as capable of lowering her inhibitions as the alcohol mentioned in the previous paragraph. But, Sally must not think so or has never considered the possibility.

The end result is Sally wrestles with the big situation in her life, but she overlooks the smaller issues fueling the bigger problem. She may admit all of them are wrong but isn't making the connection between these activities and her relationships. She sees these less flagrant activities as normal and assumes all normal people do them. She is totally unaware they are paving the way for the problem that's defeating her.

In the last chapter, we touched on Matthew 12:34-35. Let's take a closer look now. "Brood of vipers! How can you speak good things when you are evil? For the mouth speaks from the overflow of the heart. A good man produces good things from his storeroom of good, and an evil man produces evil things from his storeroom of evil." Take note of the phrase "the overflow of the heart." This verse says the choices we make in regard to how we live today are shaped by the things we chose to store up in our heart yesterday. What we stash away today will come out in the future. Our past choices become the controlling factor in our future actions.

"Out of the overflow of the heart" means our outward behavior spills over from our inward content. Our hearts become full of our lifestyle and choices, even if those choices are as subtle as what we choose to think about. Those choices are not visible now. Eventually, whatever it is we are storing internally will "overflow" and become externally visible.

Jesus taught this in the Sermon on the Mount when He said, "You have heard that it was said, **Do not commit adultery.** But I tell you, everyone who looks at a woman to lust for her has already committed adultery with her in his heart." Matthew 5:27-28 tells us every internal thought will be judged by God. If this is so, it must be because internal thoughts carry significance.

Matthew 12:34-35 specifies why they are so important. Internalizing it is the first step on the journey to doing it. What we fill our hearts with overflows into our behavior.

God expects us to stop the process at the first step. We should make a choice to fill our heart with helpful content instead of garbage. I have a good friend and mentor in the ministry who often says, "If you want to know what you are full of, watch what spills out when you get shaken up." It's a simple test, but it works.

Remember the "Dennis the Menace" comic strip? One in particular comes to mind. Dennis spent all day around town with his mom. Along the way, he passed construction workers cussing at each other, portrayed in comic strip fashion, "#*@!" He took it in. When he arrived home, he spilled it back out in conversation to his mom. In the last frame, he sat in the corner, trying to figure out what went wrong.

His heart had taken something in, which then overflowed in his own choices. He became something his mom knew better than to allow, and she corrected his course by disciplining him. In this example, the exact moral action taken in, cussing, was the immoral action that spilled out. The things stored up in the heart are most affective not by specific action, but by kind.

Matthew 12:34-35 identifies the things stored in the heart by type, such as good or evil, rather than by specific moral actions, such as lying or telling the truth. While specific actions are stored in the heart in such a way they are more likely to come back out, I also believe the verse indicates the person suffers or gains a cumulative effect based on the moral value of the action.

Thus, the total of evil stored within causes a person to be more likely to overflow with evil, making them more susceptible to evil actions that are new to them. In like manner, a person who stores up good will be more likely to do good, even if it's a good situation or opportunity they never encountered before.

Remember Sally, the illustration at the start of this chapter? The little sins feeding the problem are different than the big issue she is battling. The evil flowing out of the heart does not have to be the same specific action as the evil being stored up.

The good and evil stored up in our hearts affects us in ways other than the specific positive and negative actions we've taken. Therefore, taking positive actions in the simple, daily way we live enables us to respond better to the non-simple, uncommon circumstances and opportunities when they arrive. We can open doors of opportunity by filling our heart with positive stores. Think of them as provisions for future accomplishments.

This also explains one of the reasons why we can't get past certain struggles in our lives. We are fighting some large negative behavior and losing the battle. We don't understand why we can't beat it. Often, it's because we have a multitude of ways we're storing evil in our hearts. These other problems are of no concern to us, even though we know they're not right. We see them as small issues and ignore our wrong behavior in order to fight the battle we see as the bigger crisis. Unfortunately, the issues we see as small keep our heart full of evil and empower the greater catastrophe we are trying to overcome.

Think about an event in a crowded city. A mom gets distracted for one moment. Her baby, in its carriage, rolls down the street. It will roll into a busy intersection in a couple of seconds. If it makes it, it will be crushed, along with the child inside, by one of the numerous cars, busses, or trucks passing quickly along the road.

Three bystanders see what is about to take place. One thinks to himself, "That baby is about to get splattered. This is going to be great." This first man considers it his lucky day to see such an event.

Another thinks, "I have to stop it." This second man will even dive into traffic after it without thinking. He will risk injury or even death, but he will try to stop the carriage.

The last one thinks, "That baby is about to die. I can't stand to watch."

What assumptions did you find yourself making about these three individuals? Did you imagine how they dressed and looked? What activities do you suppose they engaged in? What patterns do you suppose each one follows in daily living? If you haven't already, pretend you are the author and round out each character.

From this one event, can we assume a whole pattern of existence and lifestyle? This pattern included a number of ways the first individual filled his life with negative things. He's most likely to be involved in harsh, destructive activities. The assumption for the second person was a pattern of living filled with positive attributes, experiences, and habits. He's more likely to be involved in noble pursuits.

It is unlikely either of these men would have formed a specific habit in regard to runaway baby carriages. But rather, they formed generic patterns toward good and evil that play out in everyday circumstances of life. Those choices for good and evil had a cumulative affect that spilled over into this unusual moment. The unusual moments of life often surprise us with our greatest opportunities for good or for evil.

Consider the baby carriage rolling toward the busy street. Which person do we want to be? Do we want to be the man who watches with amusement? Or would we rather be the one who dives after it to stop the crisis? If we want to be the second one, we must form the patterns of life which allowed him to have his heart shaped in this way. These two men did not have a chance to sit down and reason it all out morally. Instead, their reactions had to be instantaneous. Those actions that spill out of us so fast they can't be thought through reveal what we have stored in our hearts.

Let me take a moment to encourage us to be careful how we process this knowledge. We have a tendency to think that since we are aware of dangers, we can outsmart them. In this instance we would be tempted to believe we can live however we want to and still be a good person. We would like to believe we can live without heart in the little things, and somehow, we will rise up the moment bigger or more critical issues are at stake. This is very common thinking but very dangerous thinking. It never gets us around the problem; it is the problem.

In the illustration about the baby carriage, there was a third person—the one who couldn't stand to watch. This person attempts to live in the middle. They allow things into their life they know are not right. The person feels they can indulge in the little things without being affected by them. They are not totally given over to evil, but they aren't guarding their heart so they can be filled with good, either.

Their reaction was not as bad as the first person, but it was not as noble as the second person. Notice the importance of this lesson: the third person also would have allowed the child to die. Not because they delighted in it but out of a lack of positive action. No matter how much the third person wanted to be the hero, wanted to be ready to take action, the child would still be dead. Saving the child required someone whose heart was uncompromised.

The decision to fritter away the condition of our hearts over a plethora of little indulgences is also the decision to not be ready when God, our family, or the world around us needs us to be a hero. If we are going to be the person God uses to build His kingdom, we must not throw away the opportunity by believing the lie that little sins don't matter. We can be the solid rock for our families. We can provide well, faithfully train our kids, and raise outstanding citizens of heaven and earth. But this requires us to guard the storehouse of our heart with all diligence. If we want to be ready when a once in a lifetime opportunity to change the world comes along, we must not be one of the vast multitudes living with a compromised heart.

Chapter 5

Heartache begins at home

A couple of years back, I conferred with a parent. She lamented the choices of her daughter, who had become involved in Wicca. Wicca is witchcraft. Sometimes dressed up as white magic, the name change does not alter its intentions. It's a religion that seeks to control the world through spells, magic, and so on. Wicca is different from Christianity, even though some teens believe they can be both Christian and Wiccan. They are wrong and misunderstand one or both religions. Wicca is far more prevalent among teens than most parents realize.

One of the statements this mom made stuck out in my mind. She said, "We didn't raise her to be this way. We raised her to be Christian." This thought kept coming back to me, because I wondered how true it was. Through the girl's early years, both parents worked. In her early adolescence, these parents divorced. From this point on, her parental influence was as a single mom. During both periods of the girl's life, church attendance was occasional or less. I don't know if the parents were ever seen reading the Bible or praying.

The daughter had never caught the flavor of the mom's heart, or she clearly recognized the choices Mom made. She caught on to the mom's real priorities and lived according to those things she had seen modeled in her mom's patterns. The mom thought she modeled Christianity, but in reality she presented apathy toward Christianity, expressed through lack of involvement.

Thus far we have defined the heart as a storeroom. It therefore makes sense to try to control what gets stored in our hearts in order to shape our future in better ways. There are three types of stores that deserve particular attention: self-image, morality, and courage. For the next few chapters, we will discuss these attributes, beginning with self-image.

Consider how complicated it is to control what gets stored in our hearts. Our lives are full of circumstances we have no control over. Our lack of control does not change the fact our hearts are affected by them. The very first of these complicated circumstances is the family in which we were raised. As we grew up, our family was the first major contributor to the condition of our heart. Of course, no one has a perfect family, and even those few very good families have less-than-perfect moments. With the breakdown of the traditional family structure, families have become less and less prepared to build strong hearts in children. About two-thirds of the families in America are "blended" in one manner or another. Traditional families where the husband and wife married, stayed married for life, and only had kids with each other are in a solid minority. The house I was raised in was not like this, and yours probably wasn't either.

Before we jump into some of the details, let's consider two words of counsel. First, do not be discouraged by the circumstances you were raised in. They may not have been ideal, but God is able to work in our weaknesses, often better than in our strengths. We cannot look back to an unfortunate history and think we have found someone to blame for our present choices. Neither should we believe we have insurmountable barriers to our success. My second admonition is if anyone wants to understand family topics more thoroughly, then they should look for books centered on this topic. It's not in the scope of this book to delve deeply into the psychological or sociological ramifications of family life.

The household we were raised in was the first major contributor to the composition of our hearts. This is especially true in terms of our self-esteem. Whether or not we like ourselves, believe good things about ourselves, and what we expect to experience and accomplish are all shaped by our self-image. Self-esteem has a very strong effect on the heart because it is the most active part of the equation. All of us, whether we realize it or not, are constantly drawing from the store of what we think of ourselves, and by accepting what we find, we reinforce those opinions and fill our storehouse with them. If it's a negative opinion, it becomes a vicious cycle holding us back. If we cycle on a positive opinion of ourselves, we empower ourselves to constantly improve. Many books and counselors have noted anyone can choose to interrupt a destructive cycle. A short summary of how to do this would be to first identify our negative ideas about self. Next, begin stating more positive ideas, and finally, follow through with better patterns of behavior.

A simple example of this happened at a retreat the men's group of our church attended. One of the young men played a game with me. I don't know the name of the game, but it is similar to shuffleboard, only in a long and narrow raised box. In this game, the players throw the sliders by hand instead of with a stick. The first few games were close. After a while, I gained ground and almost certainly was going to win the match. At this point, I noticed a self-defeating pattern in my opponent. Right before he threw, he said aloud, "I am really bad at this game," or some similar derisive statement. I pointed this out to him. For the next couple of turns he sarcastically stated, "I am wonderful at this game!" He made a couple of throws that caused him to make a fast comeback, and he won.

If we do not challenge false or destructive self-opinions, they will hold a fierce power over us. Self-image is built into us as children, and we set a pattern of viewing ourselves positively or negatively in future situations and activities. I view myself as being good at math, reasonably adept with computers, a moderately skilled communicator, organized only in bursts, and lousy at keeping the yard clean. Every aspect of these self-formed opinions also becomes self-fulfilling. If people speak of numbers around me, I catch myself either doing the math in my head or estimating to verify if they're correct. When I need to speak in public, I can muster the courage to do so. And, of course, if anyone ever sees my yard, it won't be perfectly manicured. Not even close.

A person who achieves well almost certainly had a family who built a solid foundation under them in terms of their self-image. This occurred through a process that poured value into the person. I believe this happens when the child knows they are loved and feels the security that knowledge brings. Being loved equates to being valued. Every person perceives love at least a little bit differently, but if they can perceive it, then they will begin to see themselves as valuable and store this as self-esteem in their heart.

Notice the situation is not unilateral. First, the parents have to value and love their children. But the children also have to receive the message. This breakdown can occur because the parents are not able to love or value others, although this isn't a common situation. The failure can also occur because love and value are not communicated in a way the children understand and receive the message. The most common reason is the stress of life doesn't leave adequate time for the message to be well sent. Or, the breakdown in communicating value to a child can occur because the child is not receiving or believing the message by their own choice.

I describe this process as putting value into our kids, because if all goes well they will learn to appreciate, love, and value themselves. This value instilled in them gives their heart a solid foundation for building and storing other positive stores. For example, they can more easily see themselves as capable in a particular task if they begin with a foundation of seeing themselves as valuable and capable people.

The hardest experiences of my life were as a foster parent. A small collection of kids came through our household, ending with the son and daughter we adopted. All of these foster kids had at least one thing in common. In their first few years of life, their homes presented insecurity instead of security. Some parents were addicted to drugs and alcohol. Other parents were consumed in mental illness. Whatever the reason, the children had a hard time learning heart because they had not known security or self-value.

In training to become a foster parent, we were warned that kids who were accustomed to living in a bad environment would reject good surroundings, because they were alien to them. Insecurity was more familiar, so they found comfort in unsafe situations. One four-year-old girl riding in our car spied a policeman pulling up alongside. The policeman wasn't paying any special attention to our vehicle, other than what was normal for his duties. This girl unbuckled her seat belt and cowered down between the seats to hide while screaming at me to get away from the cop. That strange moment gave me a glimpse into how the girl was raised. Police were to be feared and run away from. The hearts that had shaped her heart were corrupt, and they formed a fearful, insecure heart in her.

Whether a child's heart forms to store value and security or fear and doubt, these foundations are shaped very early and are used to build other lessons upon them. On top of these foundations are laid moral groundwork such as what they believe is right and wrong, behavioral patterns, and the ability to achieve. If the parents are actively involved in the children's lives, they will be the primary shapers of these ideas in the hearts of their young children. It gets more complicated when the kids get older, but involved parents most often remain the primary shapers of their hearts.

The more involved we are with our kids, the better this works. The stores of the heart are caught more than they are taught. This means we put things into our children's hearts unintentionally in the course of daily life. What they observe in us, what they see us doing, and how we ourselves are built is more relevant than what we tell them.

One of the saddest facts to come out after the disaster of the Columbine High School shootings was that the perpetrators had been gathering the weapons and bombs for some time. They kept them in their bedrooms in plain sight, but their parents weren't involved enough to see the activities or devices. This is very similar to the girl involved in Wicca I mentioned at the start of this chapter.

I wish I could tell us this was a rare occurrence, but similar events have been very common. I have had this conversation with multiple parents, in regard to a number of values. Many kids are not influenced by their parents in such a way as to shape their heart. It might be they are missing the few opportunities they have to influence their children. The most important opportunities are unpredictable. Teachable moments are hard to catch. If parents miss those opportunities, they may discover even while being involved in parenting, their kids were raised with hearts completely different than what they desired to develop.

More than a few parents have been shocked after realizing what kind of person their child had become. The question they ask themselves is, "Where did that come from?" One place it comes from is media, where children are acculturated to disrespect or disregard parents. Any message a person hears over and over again becomes part of their culture. They might personally accept it or reject it. Therefore, it might not be a part of their personal worldview. Either way, it becomes a part of their culture.

They perceive it as normal because of the frequency they encounter it. Most of the time whatever they accept as normal becomes a personal practice. Disrespecting or ignoring parents is a cultural norm in our society.

Family is the first and perhaps strongest influence on the storeroom of the heart. In the first few years of life, we build a positive or negative foundation in our self-image. In the following years, all other values stored in the heart are built on those foundations. But remember, no matter how hard the past has been, God is aware and has plans for how to use us in a wonderful future.

Chapter 6

The sexualized society

Many years ago, I had some simple work done on my car. When they put it back together they accidentally left off a vacuum line. This line went to the electronic controls for the car, and the lack of its input confused the car's computer. The end result was the engine would accelerate but not decelerate. It stayed at whatever top speed it reached. After pulling onto the roadway, I noticed the car wasn't slowing down when I let off the accelerator. I bounced the accelerator pedal to the floor and up, thinking it might be stuck. This caused the engine to accelerate a little more and confirmed the pedal wasn't stuck. After a few harrowing moments, I shut it down by turning off the key.

Our immorality tends to behave like my car did. When we allow it to rev up a little, it isn't going to slow back down again. Instead, it stays at the new, faster pace unless something drastic changes the situation.

The next key concern of the heart is our moral foundation. In the technological and media savvy age we live in, there festers one moral issue that proves itself insidious. Since we live inside our culture, it's hard for us to see what is good and bad about it. We can't see the forest for the trees.

The culture and times we live in are so steeped in sexuality it is impossible for any of us to not be affected and corrupted by it. When I attended the training as a foster parent, a new word was added to my vocabulary. The word is sexualization. This happens when a child is exposed to sexual images, ideas, or activities before they are able to handle them. Scripture says the appropriate time for sexual activity is when we get married, with an intention to be married for life. Be careful not to hear this definition as saying these things begin at some age where the person is mature enough to handle sexuality. This would be a worldly viewpoint and not a scriptural one.

Children who were sexualized at a young age were far more likely to have perverse sexuality as part of their future and were less likely to have success in the normal areas of life such as family, education, and careers. In fact, they taught that it's rare for kids who are sexualized as a child to have a normal sexuality as adults. Instead, these kids are highly susceptible to dangerous behaviors such as homosexuality, promiscuity, and other society-damaging behaviors such as sexual violence or employment in the sex industry. Being exposed to sexual ideas, images, and activities causes the children to eventually delve further into sexuality than is right or healthy. This fits with what we have been learning about heart. If the heart is fed a diet of sexuality, it seeks more and more of it.

In foster care, they wanted us to watch for sexualized children, because it helped the workers to understand more about the home the children were raised in and how to help them. In the following years, I was often amazed how many homes exposed children, even preschoolers, to pornography. Even worse, some moms would bring home sexual liaisons and participate in their activities with the kids present. Even in healthier families it astounds me how kids are aware of sexual terminology from elementary school up, and increasingly younger kids are involved in sexual activity. Not many years ago, the news covered a local junior high school that had a larger pregnancy problem than the district's high school.

In these examples, we easily say these individuals are overly sexualized, and their hearts have been shaped in such a way as to cause harm. But, remember at the beginning of this chapter we were warned we cannot fairly see a situation while standing in the middle of it. Our whole society is overly sexualized and very few people, if any, have escaped it. You and I are also corrupted by over-exposure to sex.

Remember what it means to be sexualized? It means a person is exposed to sexual images, ideas, and activities that cause them to have an out of balance or perverted predisposition to sexuality. Yes, I really do mean to say sexuality out of balance—out of God's balance—is perverted, and most of us are in this boat. Our objection will be only the worst cases, like those named above, are perverted, but this an earthly perspective and not God's perspective. Unsafe sexual ideas are presented to all of us in advertising and sitcoms, but we have labeled some sexualization as normal merely because it is common. We must not make the assumption common equals normal. Common does not equal healthy.

The images and discussions on prime time television today would have only been allowed on late night TV a few years ago. If we go back a few years earlier, they weren't allowed on TV at all. If we go back a few more years, they would've only been in a few socially unacceptable magazines. A few years later, there were a multitude of such magazines, and many of these were welcomed openly in society. We are becoming sexualized, and what is normal today would have been called perverted yesterday. Those voices of yesterday were far closer to aligning with Scripture than we are today.

Before we dismiss the current line of reasoning as the rants of a puritanical fruitcake, consider how much sexual input exists in our society. We will do this by first taking a moment to discuss our sexual history and the massive media input to the problem. These factors team up to cause us to have unclean thought processes shaped by sexuality. All of this eventually leads to impure actions. To begin with, think about how our own personal history has shaped our sexual identity. I don't know your story, so I'll use mine as an example. Over forty years ago, when I grew up, a family down the street subscribed to a number of pornographic magazines. Everyone in my circle of friends knew they could visit this household when they wanted to see this kind of material. As a young boy, I wanted to view those magazines along with all of my friends. A few years later, in my junior high years, just about every young man I knew had a collection of their own magazines. Maybe they stole them from their fathers, or perhaps they obtained them when the family down the street got tired of them.

Those images of naked women affected all of us in one way or another. We will not discuss many details of those affects, leaving this material for the psychologists and doctors who know more on the subject than I do. But one aspect of it we should consider; namely, the discussions initiated by this exposure to pornography. The boys began to talk about girls in an openly sexual manner for the first time. now I know (from talking to other men) my experience was mild compared to some. Sexual talk was another form of sexual input that formed all of our histories. The reason this is significant is because, to a large extent, the speakers were making it up as they went along, while the listeners believed it. The sexual identities of these kids were built on false images because of the naiveté of youth.

This is a brief sketch of one boy's introduction to sexuality. Hopefully it illustrates that everyone has a long list of ways their sexual identities were shaped by contact with pornographic images and false information. This past input makes us more likely to recognize or seek out other sexual data. Sexuality is like the car we mentioned at the start of this chapter. After it revs up, it becomes difficult to turn off again. When it accelerates to include a new thought or activity, it maintains this thought or activity. Therefore, whatever sexual mistakes we make are likely to stay with us and be built into us. We carry them from the point of impact forward, unless something dramatic changes the pattern.

Childhood naiveté and locker room talk are not the only ways we become sexually aware. Another tremendous source of sexual input is media. Television, movies, music, print advertising, and the internet put sexual ideas into our heads. Hollywood doesn't have a clear idea of how to be funny unless it's sexually funny. Marketers have attempted to make movies more appealing to the public, not by striving for a more family friendly rating, but by adding sexual content. When MTV got its start over twenty years ago, a focus changed in music. It became important for the video to market the song as much as the musical content did. Therefore, music videos are also using sex to sell us entertainment.

Sometimes this "sex sells" approach is practiced more openly than at other times. The Food Network became one of my favorite channels. Not only do I like to cook, but on this network there wasn't a steady flow of commercials with bikini models. Unfortunately, I made reference to this from my pulpit. Almost immediately afterward, they began airing a underwear commercial in which a group of female dancers moved around the screen wearing nothing but their undergarments. The commercial may have been clever in its own way, making the statement that if the dancers were comfortable in these clothes, we would be, too. I know, and I hope you know, the advertisers used those images so the brand would stay in our mind longer because of the tight fits, exposed skin, and attractive models.

I'm not one to watch a lot of movies. At one point many years back, I was determined to find a movie and looked down the entire list of shows. In an eye-opening moment, I realized every single one was rated R or X. I know they still produce PG movies (and on rare occasions G movies), but at that moment there were none. I began to take note of how unclean movies and entertainment had become. Sexual messages are put into everything. One of the main reasons is because they work. Even if we are bound and determined to stay morally pure, our eyes will be drawn to these images, our mind will hold onto their significance, and our heart will be affected.

If we are in the habit of watching the most popular television shows, we hear a steady stream of sexual jokes. In the work place, discussion of those shows is almost inevitable. Don't be surprised if in a light-hearted moment of teasing with coworkers some of the sexual content comes out. Whatever is stored in the heart spills out at some point, even when we consider it inappropriate. Once it's out there, few people apologize and back off. Most often, it is taken for a laugh, and the comment and the subject matter become a little more socially acceptable.

After discussion in the work place becomes sexual, it tends to accelerate. In a situation like this, people find themselves having increasingly immoral discussions of sexual activity, and in the worst cases they fall into sexual affairs with co-workers. Some stop the slide into immorality before it comes to these extremes. Many others do not, and they find themselves looking back and wondering what went wrong. Very few realize the sexualized discussions were a factor. The fact their entertainment diet preceded and fueled the conversations will probably be overlooked by all of them. If they don't understand these factors pushed them to fail, they are unlikely to stop future occurrences, especially since they already experienced this particular failure.

Many people in our society consider openness to sexuality as healthy and enlightened. They indulge themselves in a steady stream of pornography or sexual encounters. They end up participating in behaviors and practices they found reprehensible at the outset. Maybe it will be child pornography. When they first started, the idea disgusted them, but when images of adults stopped thrilling them, they moved on to stronger medicine. Some of these individuals will move on to sexual contact with children. Others find themselves moving on to homosexuality, because they are no longer satisfied with heterosexual relationships.

Since sexualization is progressive, a person who wants to be strong hearted must be very concerned with how they view and process sexual images and data. As a rule of thumb, we cannot believe what we hear about sex. (Rules of thumb are not always true; there are exceptions.)

I commented earlier that the pre-teen boys' discussion about sex was dangerous, because the speakers were lying, and the listeners believed the lies only because of their inexperience. The most sexually damaged young men were not the ones telling lies in the locker room. They were the ones who left the locker room and acted on those lies. They believed what they heard and made it real when they did what the first young man had only thought about.

This is true with adults, too. The best example I can give is in regard to research. A number of years ago, a landmark book released, claiming to have scientifically researched sex.[1] Everyone read the book, and everyone believed it. Many credit this book with starting the sexual revolution. This first book was followed by a second, and many refer to them both as the Kinsey reports.[2]

Years later, it's known the researchers were biasing their research. Their numbers were not realistic.[3] This falsehood is further complicated by the fact that one of their most commonly quoted statistics isn't in their materials. The percentage of individuals who are homosexual is commonly reported to be about 10 percent based upon the findings of the Kinsey reports. Not only is the real number much lower, but Kinsey never made this claim. (Remember my rule of thumb; we cannot believe what we hear about sex.) As a response to their published findings, many people responded by believing what was published and trying things they otherwise would not have done. Therefore the lie, at least to some degree, shaped public activity.

However, the lies we are told openly are not as dangerous as the lies implied to us over and over again. These lies become part of the culture, and we believe them to be normal and correct because of repeated exposure. Let's list some of the lies that gained ground in our society over the past few years:

1. Homosexuality is normal, and homosexuals have committed, long-term relationships just like married heterosexual couples.

2. Oral sex does not count as having lost one's purity and is often practiced by kids who want to remain virgins.

3. Sex is the greatest single right of any human being, and this right is protected constitutionally under the right to privacy. As a corollary to this, parents have no right to know about or to interfere with a child's sexual activities.

4. Every woman leans toward lesbianism, and since all men are perverts, movement in this direction is justified.

5. The age of consent is outdated and should be legally removed or reduced.

This is a short list of the lies commonly endorsed today. Don't be confused; they are listed here as non-truths. We've probably heard at least one of these messages in the last twenty-four hours. Whether they came from the news media or entertainment, they are popular lies to tell. The sheer volume of these false ideas overwhelms common sense.

One aspect of this problem—which will hit our society very hard—is how these lies and a multitude of others have been told to the next generation. The most sexually charged shows on TV are not shows produced for adults, but those for teenagers and pre-teens. The greatest amount of sexual lying aims at those who are least prepared to sort it out. Many parents would be shocked by the amoral values some shows and networks are teaching their teens.

If we try to find out what teens and young adults believe in the area of sexual ethics, we will find a frighteningly large variation from the values of the rest of society. What they consider normal behavior is a distance beyond what their parents expect, even if their parent's moral foundations are extreme compared to society as a whole. To compound the problem, these kids have been sold on the idea they're standing on the moral high ground, older adults just don't understand, and keeping these issues private from their parents stands as the wisest course of action. Even kids who seem to be grounded in church are buying into the lies being fed to them by media, society, and those with their own sexual agendas. Church attendance one day a week will not protect our children while the voice of society rages at them seven days a week. Under these conditions, why would we expect them to trust God's Word rather than the much louder voice they hear day in and day out?

I commented in chapter five about parents not knowing what factors are shaping their kids' hearts. The sexual input our kids receive is far more than most of us realize, and I believe it is far more detrimental than my generation encountered. If we accept the heart is a storeroom and immoral behavior causes a person to be unable to live and achieve with heart, then it stands to reason our world is going downhill with each succeeding generation as they tumble further and further into sexualization.

---

1 Alfred C. Kinsey, Wardell C. Pomeroy, and Clyde E. Martin, *Sexual Behavior in the Human Male* (Philadelphia, PA: W.B. Saunders Company, 1948)

2 Alfred C. Kinsey, Pomeroy, Martin, & Gebhard, *Sexual Behavior in the Human Female* (Philadelphia, PA: W.B. Saunders Company, 1953)

3 Judith A. Reisman, PHD, *Sexual Sabotage* (Washington, DC: WND Books, 2010)

Chapter 7

Stifling God's blessing

Perhaps some readers think this book resembles *Chicken Little*, causing a stir over things that aren't really a problem. We must make the careful and correct decision not to trivialize how the sexual input around us compromises our hearts. This is a real issue, and we need to motivate ourselves to take it seriously. In order to accomplish this, consider several examples of how God responded when a culture became overly sexualized.

The obvious place to begin is with Sodom and Gomorrah. Lot and Abraham head their separate ways. Lot goes in the direction presenting the best opportunities in the form of pasturelands. Somehow, this herdsman ends up living right in the middle of town—a town God is about to destroy because of its immorality. We are not told what immorality took place there, but we do get examples of it when God sends messengers to warn Lot to clear out. The men in town take special notice of the messengers and want to have sex with them. They are willing to commit acts of violence in order to accomplish this objective.

Don't let familiarity cause us to skip over this without noticing the details. They want to have forced sex, group sex, with strangers of the same gender. This desire wasn't a passing thought. It was an action they became intent upon. They were so determined that they were ready and prepared for whatever violence it took to accomplish it.

Another glimpse of how sexually perverted the situation had become is discovered in the compromise Lot offered these men. In his desire to protect his guests, he offered to send his daughters out for the crowd to abuse. I can't help but wonder what thought went through the minds of the young girls when they heard their father offer them to appease the crowd. Few actions in the Bible are harder to understand than this offer made by Lot. We might assume it was the result of their patriarchal society, where women and girls were of no value. Be wise and insightful, rather than dismissive, because when a society considers women to be property, this is proof it has become sexually tainted. In the short period of time since Lot moved there, he'd become part of the town's awful culture.

While looking at this event, it's also worth noting the men had no interest in the girls. Instead, they were determined to have the visitors for their perversions. They not only wanted to have sex with other men, they'd lost all interest in females. This is one of the outcomes of sexualization. Men and women leave the natural sexual desire for the opposite gender and desire their own gender. Paul warns us about this possibility in Romans 1:26-27. "This is why God delivered them over to degrading passions. For even their females exchanged natural sexual intercourse for what is unnatural. The males in the same way also left natural sexual intercourse with females and were inflamed in their lust for one another. Males committed shameless acts with males and received in their own persons the appropriate penalty for their perversion." As I previously noted, continuing down the road of ungodly sexuality will bring us to destinations we never intended to visit. Sodom and Gomorrah was a place so far down the moral road, God knew they would not return and destroyed them in order to prevent the spread of their influence.

For another example of how sexuality affects the heart, consider the long battle with Baal worship in the period of the Divided Kingdom. Baal worship was a form of idolatry centered on fertility. The god Baal and his female counterpart, Ashteroth, were thought to increase the fertility of families, flocks, and fields if they were pleased. The fact their practices were idolatry was serious enough. God described idolatry as spiritual adultery. But this form of idolatry seemed to have greater power than other false gods. Other forms of idolatry, such as the worship of Molech, were less persistent. Baal worship kept coming back.

The reason it persisted was Baal was highly sexual. One of the ways a man was to worship or serve these false gods was to go to their temple and have sex with a temple prostitute. This false worship had a natural appeal to the Israelites. Since sexual sin has a very persistent nature, Baal worship tended to stay in Israel until some dramatic, drastic action took place. The fall of Jerusalem was the final drastic action God used to eradicate Baal worship from His people. The majority of the survivors were hauled off to another land until those who returned had no familiarity with this immorality. Meanwhile, the few survivors who remained in Israel were cleansed of these practices by a series of wars.

Consider the fall of the Roman Empire. One way to view the end of the Roman Empire is it collapsed because of immorality. The citizens became so entangled with sensual pleasure they weren't prepared for anything else. When bigger threats loomed, they weren't ready to buckle down and sacrifice in order to preserve their way of life. As a result, they were swept away along with their licentiousness.

A couple of weeks before writing this, I was listening to a Christian radio program—*Focus on the Family*—when I heard David Wheaton, their guest, say, "Your theology or your philosophy always follows your morality."[1] David is an author who wrote a book about how higher education undermines Christianity. He specifically wrote about the trend of when a Christian student starts attending a secular college, he or she almost always loses their solid foundation within a short period of time. It is a remarkable pattern with great strength. If it continues on the scale it's moving in, it will be a major threat to the existence of Christianity in America.

The specific discussion was *how* the college experience undermines the faith of participants. The author directed our attention to the initial experience of the mandatory coed freshman dorm. The vast majority of colleges require freshmen to live in the dorm. In secular universities, those dorms are largely unsupervised coed dorms. The college experience has always been one of getting out of the house and experimenting with newfound freedoms. This experimentation takes on a whole new level in a coed dorm. Since most young adults in America are not bound by the morality of faith, sexual freedom becomes quite open in the dorm. People who truly try to honor God may turn away from these things at first, but turning away becomes difficult when it manifests itself all the time.

One determined young lady spoke with me about the difficulty of turning away from something she faced on every side. She said she found it nearly impossible to get away from immorality in the dorms when she had to have a roommate. When I asked why the roommate was important, she explained that even though she attempted to maintain a degree of discretion, her roommate still invited men into the room, sometimes to stay overnight. She ended up having several roommates, because when she found one who expressed similar moral values, the person ended up making a moral shift, and the problem would reoccur.

In a situation such as this, David Wheaton made the assertion secular colleges undermine Christian beliefs. They may not purposely do so, but they accomplish as much by placing a person in a situation with extreme sexual temptations. Then, when the person falls for those temptations, the activity they're involved in re-shapes their thinking about right and wrong. It was in this context the author stated, "Your theology or your philosophy always follows your morality." This is the basic lesson of heart in this book. It may be a rewording of it. It may focus on one direction of the flow between heart and action, but it still cuts to the root principle.

One of the important truths of heart is moral failures in our lives do not remain isolated in one arena. Moral failures spread like a contagion into other parts of our lives and into other areas of immorality. These acts cause us to become unlikely to act valorously when we come across a critical moment or lifetime opportunity.

People mistakenly believe their sexual patterns do not affect the rest of their life. It's common to believe they are private and no one will ever know. Recently, a man working in law enforcement took his own life when he realized he was about to be arrested on child pornography charges. It is obviously not true our sexual sins remain private.

Earlier I discussed how self-image was one of the most important stores in the storeroom of the heart. In this chapter and the previous chapter, we've discussed how sexualization has affected our society. Let's wrap up this point by drawing back from the discussion of sexual immorality to all forms of immorality.

Our morality is stored in our heart. If our storeroom is full of immoral actions, we feel bad about ourselves and accentuate the problem by storing not only immorality, but also a bad self-image. None of us feel good about or think well of ourselves while doing things we know are wrong.

Remember when coaches forbade smoking, drinking, girls, movies, and similar things because they took the player's focus away from the game? Perhaps those coaches knew what they were talking about. Our world has gone through a shift of its moral standards, and in this shift we've incorporated false ideas that prevent us from ever being fully on our game. In the worst cases, we can't break away long enough to carry out the daily responsibilities of life.

Let's link the moral slide of society to another shift taking place. When I was in the latter part of elementary school, just about everyone I knew dreamed of becoming a rock star. They wanted to learn to play instruments, write songs, and be discovered by a record producer who serendipitously got lost in their neighborhood and heard them practicing in the garage. We were young, and this type of fantasy thinking was easy. By the time I was in high school, the musically talented had practiced hours each week for several years. Most of the rest of us moved on to prepare for some other direction, career, or goal. We found other interests and became somewhat realistic about what it would take to accomplish our goals in life.

Right now, among the older teens and young adults I know a surprisingly large number expect to get a career in sports, music, acting, modeling, or some similar endeavor. Most have no practice, no discipline for improving their skills, and no plan to bring about their goal. Basically, they live with fantasies they should have abandoned at a younger age. I know a large number who have no idea how to move forward with reasonable goals and cannot figure out why they aren't making progress. These individuals have the everyday version of the problem we've been discussing. The storehouse of their heart was never filled with the courage, work ethic, or the moral values necessary to move forward in real life.

Some of the cultural trends shaping our society include adult children returning home to live with parents, children being raised by grandparents instead of parents, and people frequently switching jobs and careers. These trends are blamed on the economy or addiction rates or a number of other factors. I'm concerned these issues may be precipitated not so much by these problems as by the de-motivation people feel when their hearts have been repeatedly weakened. Other reasons play into these situations, but maybe the corporate heart of a nation is the greatest driving force for its economy, for its addiction rate, and for the health of its families.

As a nation, we accomplish less because we are a disheartened people. We are brokenhearted by everything from drugs to divorces to sexualization and a whole lot more. Behind all of these negative factors resides a morally compromised society which hasn't made the connection between its choices and the problems they create. We've spent a lot of time on the sexualization of our society, because it's likely to be the single greatest factor in keeping us brokenhearted. But sexualization is only one example of the immorality permeating our society.

First and foremost, we need to admit all of this immorality exists. We are all affected by it. It is out of balance with God's will, and it puts our hearts out of balance. We stifle God's ability to bless us and use us by overlooking the problems of our own immoral culture.

---

1 David Wheaton, *University of Destruction* (Minneapolis, MN: Bethany House, 2005)

Chapter 8

The self-image conundrum

One of the issues we must face when discussing heart is discouragement. Just like self-image and morality, courage is a primary store of the heart. Everyone on this planet has moments when they are encouraged or heartened. At these times, it feels like we can accomplish anything. We also have times of discouragement or times when our hearts are broken. At these times, it can feel as if we are incapable of doing anything worthwhile. The destructive power of a broken heart becomes so strong it can even feel as if we are internally dead.

When we refer to discouragement as the equivalent of a broken heart, we need to be careful. Our current colloquial use of the term "broken-hearted" almost always denotes an emotionally based term for when a relationship has ended. We would be better off looking at it in a fuller way. Certainly the ending of a relationship discourages us, but many other things break our heart as well. Life is full of disappointments. Distresses such as the loss of a job or a severe illness (and the realization of our own mortality) also break our hearts. Life is full of hurts. Any one of these hurts can be a heart breaker in the sense of undermining our moral courage.

A broken heart, or discouragement, makes us less able to achieve, less likely to do the right things, and more vulnerable to temptation. Discouragement makes us weak in heart, not just in the emotional sense, but in the sense our moral fiber becomes weakened. It is important to accept and understand how difficult events in life also damage our hearts.

When we look through the book of Proverbs, it is easier to find verses on disappointment and heartache than it is to find verses on relationships. We might expect these other issues we have discussed—family struggles and the sexualization of society—would be more prominent. But verses discussing good old-fashioned discouragement are common. A collection of hurts we think of as minor issues may be the greatest source of discouragement in our lives. Consider Proverbs 12:25, "Anxiety in a man's heart weighs it down, but a good word cheers it up." This passage defines worry as a heart issue. We don't want to imply a person of heart walks blindly through life without taking concern over the struggles they encounter. When our life overflows with concerns, weighs down our heart a little bit more with each one. Enough of these small stresses and our heart will be overcome not by the big issues of life, but by the multiplication of little issues.

Think about what this means for the times we live in. The stresses of daily life may not be larger than those of past years, but they certainly are more numerous. To use one example, consider what it means to have a boat. The boat promises to make life more fun, give the family time together, and improve their standard of living. But the boat likely came with a boat payment. It may be a huge issue or a minor one to make the payment, but either way it adds an additional worry. The payment is just the beginning. We also have to carve out time to use the boat, or we wasted money buying it. Then, we have to get people to cover our other responsibilities while we're on the boat. And, of course, it would be best if we learned some basic boating safety. Make sure the kids pack the right supplies, plan lunch and snacks, and verify everyone has a fishing pole and knows how to use it. Finally, the boat needs fresh fuel and all the proper maintenance completed.

I know these are all small stressors, but it isn't the weight of each one we are commenting on. It's the combined effect of them all together. Each one weigh down the heart a little bit more. We can easily get used to these issues. We will have a stronger heart if we do. Don't forget they weigh on us, especially when they are new. This explains why people take on a boat, jet ski, ATV, or RV and are grumpy when they start using it. It's the worry of all of those new stressors making them carry extra weight and feel additional pressure. If they overcome the difficulty of the moment, they benefit from added heart in the future. If they give in to the stress of the early attempts, they might become broken-hearted and shy away from using the new toy. If they do, every time they pass the gadget in the garage, they reinforce the failure.

Worry is probably the smallest example of heartbreak I could be citing from Proverbs. The next passage I would call our attention to is Proverbs 13:12. "Delayed hope makes the heart sick, but fulfilled desire is a tree of life." This proverb contrasts "delayed hope" and its result with "fulfilled desire" and the opposite result. In the first part, our heart becomes sick. The latter part has positive benefits, described as "a tree of life." We should keep in mind we are people of want. Regardless of who we are, we always want something. It's not always bad to want something. God built into us a desire to achieve and excel.

As a rule of thumb, when we want an object, we have to be wary of materialism and its destructive power. Our society must always seek to sell us a new toy or gadget. I've developed a personal habit I use to curb impulse spending. I attempt to wait before buying. Only if I still want it after a suitable wait will I seriously consider a purchase. Without a rule like this, my life would be full of cool gadgets. Many would add payments to my budget. I would seldom or never use most of them. And all of them would weigh down my heart and affect my ability to achieve.

However, when we want an accomplishment, it is often a good thing that strengthens us in the future. Examples of these types of desires would be: educational goals, such as getting a master's degree; career opportunities, such as being selected for a promotion; hopes for our children, such as seeing them excel in sports or academics; or even smaller personal goals, such as some kind of fitness goal or memorizing Scripture. These types of desires still need to be managed, and sometimes we have to wait for the right time to pursue them.

Whether it is an object or an accomplishment we are seeking, the verse says not getting it makes us "heart sick." This means we become discouraged at a deep level. When we set a goal in our lives and are working toward something we really want, we become very invested in the pursuit. If this achievement delays, or worse yet, the possibility is completely lost, it affects our heart. Few things are as discouraging as realizing we will never get something we've been striving for. We can be deeply shaken by the time spent on the project, the costs paid in the pursuit, and the disappointment of not having what consumed our imaginations and desires.

On the other side of the coin, getting something we've been working toward strengthens our hearts. This verse describes it as a "tree of life," which is contrasted with "makes the heart sick." We will address this more fully in a later chapter on accumulating courage. If our choices lead to a string of accomplishments, we build courage into our hearts, preparing ourselves to be ready for great opportunities. Life is good when we are able to accomplish meaningful things. This is where we find the life God intends for us. Therefore, a "fulfilled desire is a tree of life." Of course, we should notice it's possible to desire things that in the long run, or even in the short run, will harm us. These are things like an extra-marital affair or an unreasonable amount of clout. Of course, these are not the things this verse refers to.

Disappointments, even though they are a normal part of life, are a special concern of heart. Since they affect us in a manner deeper than what shows on the surface, we should be careful to manage what we desire. There are people objecting, "We can't control what we want." This belief isn't true. We can, and we must. Saying we can't is the petty excuse of a person who is undisciplined. At a deep level, this person believes being out of control of their emotions is the easiest way to get what they want. Being a person of heart means mastering our emotions, and therefore we manage our wants. Learning to want only what is truly good for us is a normal and healthy discipline mature adults need to have. This skill gives us a powerful tool for building heart.

Please be sure to understand I'm not encouraging us to be devoid of wants. Some desires are healthy. Ambition and motivation are born of the desire to accomplish, and these things are good, healthy, and necessary to be a person of heart. Be careful which desires we allow to drive us. Analyze whether or not what we want is healthy. When considering whether a desire is healthy, be sure to think about every aspect of health, including whether it is spiritually healthy. No matter how humanly good something is, if it's outside of God's will, then it is spiritually unhealthy.

Before we leave the topic of encouragement and its effect on the heart, let's discuss suggestions on what to do and not do in regard to encouragement. First, consider Proverbs 27:9, "Oil and incense bring joy to the heart, and the sweetness of a friend is better than self-counsel." This passage tells us we can use our surroundings, our five senses, and our social contacts as sources of encouragement.

In regards to surroundings, our environment affects our attitude. If our living and work spaces are clean and well kept, we stand a better chance of staying encouraged. When we live in a perpetual mess (or if your desk looks like mine), we must work harder to get past discouragements. Another aspect of surroundings is whether we allow ourselves to get out and about. Being in one setting day in and day out affects us, even if it is the most pleasant of places. We should allow ourselves to have an occasional change of scenery as a means of prompting encouragement.

The verse says to use our senses to bring joy to the heart. The reference to "oil and incense" is best understood as pleasant aromas and tactile sensations. The incense mentioned was like perfume to scent the air as it burned. The oil was likely anointing oil or soothing balm. Not only was physical touch encouraged, but they used oil to enhance the experience of touch. One of the ways to find encouragement is to fill our senses in pleasant ways, assuming the pleasure is found in moral behavior. Doing things we know are immoral to try to improve our encouragement or our self-esteem always backfires. We will never feel good about doing things we know are wrong.

The final way to find encouragement in this passage is to spend time with friends. Being social, even for an introvert, will often be a deeply encouraging time. Friends can draw us out and lift us up in wonderful ways. Notice "sweetness of a friend" is held in contrast to "self-counsel." I believe the verse is not only telling us the presence of a friend is good but accepting the counsel of friends is also good. Other people can often see a situation fairly when we are too close to know the truth about it. Sometimes, we just can't see the forest for the trees.

If it's true we are to seek the counsel of friends and not to rely on our own opinion, then we should avoid isolation. Social isolation is a problem, but isolation of ideas is a big part of why it is dangerous. We must never believe we are the only ones who can see the truth. A wise person has friends who are able to serve as counselors.

This is reflected in Proverbs 15:30. "Bright eyes cheer the heart; good news strengthens the bones." The words "bright eyes" at the beginning of the verse refers to being around other people who are cheerful. Being around people who are having good, clean fun encourages us, while being alone with our own misery discourages us. These cheerful people speak in positive, uplifting ways. This is why the latter portion of the verse says, "good news strengthens the bones."

Another tool to control discouragement is to not feed the negatives of a bad situation. Proverbs 25:20 says, "Singing songs to a troubled heart is like taking off clothing on a cold day or like pouring vinegar on soda." Simplifying what the verse says, sad songs sung to a troubled heart make matters worse. Think about the kind of music the average teenager listens to. It's music filled with negative emotion. A hopeless rage is portrayed in the style of the music, and the subject matter is often laced with sadness. Little wonder why teen angst has such a powerful hold. Honestly, some people never seem to outgrow it.

The thought many people have is that sad or angry songs help us deal with negative emotions by expressing how we feel. When the emotion is expressed, it allows the hearer to let out those emotions. This line of reasoning made sense until compared with the truth of this Scripture. Focusing on a disappointment keeps it alive and gives it energy. Sad songs have this effect of not letting the person move forward and get past the hurt. It's the equivalent of wallowing in the moment. Real progress means learning to move forward and to get past the pain.

In order to move forward, we need to have some way to express those hurts, but this expression is always most accurate when it comes from inside ourselves. A sad song or the feedback of a counselor may express similar feelings, but these external forms of emotional input will never be adequate for our personal hurt. Proverbs 14:10 says, "The heart knows its own bitterness, and no outsider shares in its joy." Even if a sad song helps to release emotions stuck inside us, they won't be accurate enough to complete the process. We have to find closure for ourselves. Sad songs, movies, or stories may initiate this search, but they cannot be used to replace it.

Consider an illustration why sad songs don't help us overcome a problem. No matter what else we allow our mind to think about, do not think about a submarine. Of course, the problem is that the minute we mention the submarine, it becomes planted in our mind. What we attempt not to think about is given power by the request to not think about it.

It's the same with negative emotions. We get stuck in them and wallow. Instead of seeking to learn from the situation and get back on our feet, we become paralyzed by the circumstance. Getting over discouragement requires we put it behind us. One mistake is to set it aside without learning the lessons God wants to teach us in the situation. The more common mistake is to become stranded in the pain, unable to move forward.

Encouragement and discouragement are special concerns of anyone who wishes to live as a person of heart. Managing our own encouragement is difficult, but if we are able to remain encouraged it greatly empowers our ability to achieve. For one last verse on the subject, consider Proverbs 15:15. "All the days of the oppressed are miserable, but a cheerful heart has a continual feast." This passage contrasts a negative state and its result with a positive attitude and its result. The negative situation is "the days of the oppressed," which is contrasted with "a cheerful heart." In order for these two to stand in opposition, the oppression must not be external. It must be talking about the internal oppression a discouraged person feels. The results are "miserable," contrasted with "a continual feast." This image of a feast describes happy, celebrative emotions.

This is exactly what it is like to be a person of encouragement; it's like living within a continuous celebration. If we keep ourselves encouraged, it will be a solid step toward being a person of heart. For this reason, we should consider the issues we allow to become heart desires. Seeking after meaningful things may be a large part of accumulating courage and building our heart. However, seeking after worthless things only signs us up for heartbreaks, and none of us can afford to take them lightly.

Chapter 9

When our heroes are criminals

In the course of this discussion we have now reached an important point. We must decide if we agree the heart is important. We must decide if our disregard for the content of our hearts is a central part of what's wrong with our society. We will move on to discuss solutions, but before we can talk about those, we should decide if this issue is genuine or not. Only after admitting these issues are real will we be able to deal with them. If we read this entire book but never wrestle with whether we agree and are personally corrupted by the heartless society around us, we stop short of gaining the most benefit.

In the first chapter, we heard the story of a high school football team that turned around a losing streak by the power of heart. This event caused me to consider and do a Bible study on what it meant to have heart. In telling us about this team, the statement was made the team had been fighting an internal battle, and only after the internal battle was won would external battles be won as well. Putting the cards flat on the table, I meant for the discussion of this book to create an internal battle in us. We need to come to the point where we wrestle with ourselves about the small things in our lives we thought weren't important. To become a person of heart, we have to admit this little stuff is important. What was true for the football team is true for us, too. We will only win external battles after the internal battle is over. The major attributes of character are formed in a multitude of small choices.

Here are some of my basic assertions. What any individual is capable of accomplishing is dependant upon the content they have stored inside their heart. The negative input of our times, our subtle compromises with culture, our sexualization by society, and the wreckage of our personal lives have corrupted our hearts to such an extent our whole society is moving in a disastrous direction. We are carried along in this current and are not accomplishing all God has for us because of it.

If we can affirm these statements, then we are ready for the remaining chapters, where we will discuss the redirecting of our hearts. But before we do, let's fuel the fire some more.

Every society needs heroes. These are people we admire and emulate. When technology progressed to the point it could create media, our entertainment produced fictional heroes. Their images continue to shape the heart of our culture and reflect the heart of our society. These heroes influence the people who encounter them, shaping society. They reflect the shape of society, because their design is a product of the culture and times they are created in.

The survivors of World War II have been called the greatest generation that ever lived. They were extreme times that created strong-hearted people. In June of 1938, a hero was introduced by DC Comics.[1] His ideals were to fight for "truth, justice, and the American way." He was clean cut, honest, and had no skeletons in his closet. Superman became an icon and shaped generations of young men who desired to live the life of a hero. I don't mean to say those times were idyllic, but they produced a positive role model.

Some of us may say we've overlooked a great deal of the character development of Superman. When we hold him up in this way, we overlook the *Superman* movies where the hero behaved in other ways. In a sense this proves our point. In order to modernize the character and make him suitable for these times, they portrayed him less nobly. He stepped down from his role as superhero in order to have a relationship with his love interest. This plot line was a development drawn from the time in which it was created. The original character would never put his interests above the needs of others. He cared more about the needs of others than his own desires and comforts. When the movies were produced, the common definition of good changed. People believed sexual gratification was a sufficient justification for stepping away from responsibilities. Superman did this. But notice that Superman had to go back and undo the damage wrought by His disastrous choice in the movie.

The original Superman reflected what a hero should be. Someone we lift up and point to, someone we desire to emulate. If we portray them as unrealistically good, then so be it. This provides us with a higher calling to strive for in our society.

But our society desires another type of hero. Heroes now must always have some kind of skeleton in their closet. We prefer tormented heroes with a dark side guiding them through their days. Addressing this issue, media analyst Brent Bozell, said, "Why can't a show like *Heroes* be pitched . . . as a straightforward superhero story without the creepy dark themes that seem to be strictly enforced as if there were some sort of pro-creepiness Hollywood union rule? Obviously, the dirty word in today's Hollywood is 'innocence.' A show that resembles an old-fashioned comic book would be scorned as hopelessly retrograde."[2]

If we have not taken notice of it, let's not miss noticing it now. A multitude of shows indicate the way to fight evil is to invoke evil. A startling number of shows attempt to provide heroes who use magic or witchcraft to defeat evil. They assume not all things evil are actually bad, and being in touch with our dark side is a necessary compromise in order to be a modern day hero. We could name a large number of shows, movies, books, and comics operating on this principle.

In order to explain how bad the situation is, let me point to the character named Hellboy. Hellboy is a relatively modern creation who first appeared in comic books in 1993.[3] He became more popular through a 2004 movie. Animated movies are in production, and sequels to the movie are coming.

Hellboy is a fictional character with a fictional history. As a means of understanding how different this hero is, we should learn about his past. He is a demon brought to earth by a Nazi plot seeking to regain control of World War II, shortly before the fall of Germany. What they conjured up was not a violent, adult demon; he turned out to be a baby demon. Hellboy was liberated by United States soldiers and brought to a secret base in New Mexico where they raised him. He is portrayed as a gruff adult demon, dangerous only to enemies. He works with a group called the Bureau for Paranormal Research and Defense (BPRD), defending mankind from occultist evils. He is red, has a tail, and would have horns if he didn't whittle them down. Especially interesting is his right hand. It's made of stone. It is called the Hand of Doom and is somehow going to be responsible for bringing about the apocalypse.

How did we get from Superman to Hellboy? I suggest the major reason is the society that birthed Superman looked at the character from Krypton and thought, "That is so great." Today, society looks at a character like Hellboy and thinks, "That is so cool." The individuals who created Superman and the people who idolized him would be repulsed by Hellboy. Meanwhile, the individuals who are attracted to Hellboy look at Superman as an outdated relic—a character whose ideals and behavior are boring. This choice is a reflection of the times, and the times reflect the heart of our society.

Isaiah 5:20 says:

> Woe to those who call evil good and good evil,
> who substitute darkness for light and light for darkness,
> who substitute bitter for sweet and sweet for bitter.
> Woe to those who are wise in their own opinion and clever in their own sight.

This verse speaks of people who get so far into a moral slide everything they look at is opposite. Evil is good. Darkness is light. Bitter is sweet. They have the right to form their opinions about things, and they intend to use the privilege to its fullest. Some invoke the privilege of definition so fully it has become more important than truth. Many people care more about being original than about being right. What is cool is more important than what is healthy or morally correct.

If we are a society that elevates a demon as a hero, perhaps we have also become people who call darkness light and light darkness. Maybe we've become so accustomed to storing up evil things in our hearts evil things now look good to us. Evil is what we are familiar with, drawn to, and more likely to imitate. When we become this acclimated to evil, good begins to be seen differently as well. Notice in the verse it doesn't just say, "evil for good," "darkness for light," and "bitter for sweet," but it also says "good for evil," "light for darkness," and "sweet for bitter." This is very important to catch, because it's one problem for people to say some particular bad choice is okay. This means they are simply misguided, not understanding the action is wrong. It is another thing altogether to recognize people have switched the places of wrong and right completely. This is not being misguided; this is being totally perverted.

When a person has a backward perspective on right and wrong, it is exceptionally difficult for them to straighten out again. We can correct people who are misguided or naïve about wrong by showing them how the wrong does damage to them or to society around them. In this manner, we are showing them why wrong is wrong. When one is perverted to the point they see right and wrong backward, we can't merely show them why something is wrong. If we do, the wrong results we point to will only be seen by their perverted eyes as right results.

This is similar to what happens in our society with sexually active teenagers. In times past, parents and other moral guides could point to the likelihood of having a baby as a wrong result, which they should avoid by abstaining from wrong behavior. Today there are a startling number of teens who look at the baby as a reward, as a positive outcome. One could point to sexually transmitted disease, but some teens look at this as a badge of honor. Point to the very real possibility of death, and these same people may shock us even more by referring to dying young as a legacy worth seeking. They remember how for many years, from James Dean to Kurt Cobain, our culture has celebrated and elevated those who live bright and burn out fast.

So here is the final fuel for the fire we are looking for; we can make a personal choice now to turn around. Now, while we can still see the difference between right and wrong. Or, we can wait until the perversion of our hearts, and likewise of our society, has progressed to the point where turning is impossible. When we offer this choice, please do not look at the rest of the world around us as we make a decision. Our own heart is the only one we are responsible for. We must make personal decisions for ourselves first. Only after we've made a decision for ourselves will we be able to influence others. We already have enough leaders who believe they can ignore their own failures and guide others out of a life of mediocrity.

This is the exact type of hypocrisy Jesus condemned in the Pharisees. The decision we make must first be a decision for ourselves. Will we decide to unleash the full potential of our heart by controlling what we allow to be stored there?

If we are answering with a bold yes, then read on. The remainder of this book will give us some great tools in fulfilling this commitment.

---

1 "Superman," Wikipedia, last modified April 27, 2012, http://en.wikipedia.org/wiki/Superman

2 Brent Bozell, "overheard," *Plugged In* (March 2007): 12

3 "Hellboy," *Wikipedia*, last modified April 23, 2012, http://en.wikipedia.org/wiki/Hellboy

Chapter 10

Blessed with a heart transplant

It's our intention to have the kind of heart God can use in powerful ways. We can build in ourselves a heart God uses to shape societies, to bring people eternally into His family, and to guide history forward. If we want to be people whose lifetime accomplishments overshadow the norm, then we must accept this truth: to be a person who accomplishes above the norm, we must also be a person who lives above the norm.

We desire to learn how to live above the mediocrity and compromise ensnaring most the world. We also want to learn to go beyond average and to set aside all comparisons to others in order to allow Christ to direct our lives. A person who unleashes the power of heart must not be doing well by the world's standard but must be living according to God's standard, God's discipleship, and God's unique call on their life.

If we succeed in this goal, it is likely the journey the Lord leads us on will be different than the life experienced by any other person. There is only one George Washington. His path through lesser battles, then through the Revolutionary War, his path through prayer and Scripture, his path through the first presidency of the United States was unlike anyone else's path. There is only one King David. David's life journey through shepherding sheep, private worship and hymn writing, facing Goliath and the Philistines, and becoming king of Israel was uniquely his own. Our life stories will be our own too. We dare not say it won't be of equal value to society and history as these others great leaders. We don't know what God has planned for us, but we know it is possible that He has influential intentions for us and our lives.

Even though our journeys are different, I firmly believe the greatest hearts of history had the same starting place. This starting place is when they gave their heart completely and absolutely over to God. In previous chapters, we learned about all the ways our world makes it hard for us to have a quality heart. If we are honest, we will admit the situation adds up to the conclusion none of us are capable of turning our lives around. We cannot choose to overcome the input of this world, because the onslaught of sinful ideas stored in our hearts is constant and devastating. Despite the effects of our sexualization, our discouragement, and our broken families, we should not give up hope.

The good news Jesus came to give us is this: where our ability is lacking, His ability is abundant. God can do in us what we cannot do in ourselves. God delivered a promise to us twice through the writings of the prophet Ezekiel. The two instances are in Ezekiel 11:18-21 and 36:24-28. Let's dissect the first of these two instances. "'When they arrive there, they will remove all its detestable things and all its abominations from it. And I will give them one heart and put a new spirit within them; I will remove their heart of stone from their bodies and give them a heart of flesh, so they may follow My statutes, keep My ordinances, and practice them. Then they will be My people, and I will be their God. But as for those whose hearts pursue their desire for detestable things and abominations, I will bring their actions down on their own heads.' This is the declaration of the Lord GOD." The second sentence says God will give these people a heart transplant. The heart in them now is hardened to the point it's described as a heart of stone. God will pull the hardened heart out and replace it with a soft, new heart made of flesh, as it should be.

The single greatest change that can take place in us is brought about by God and not by ourselves, because it's beyond our ability to make. God's grace, His very nature, is to offer us what we need when we can't achieve it for ourselves. It is a total remaking of ourselves from the inside out. Beyond our ability is an understatement; it's more accurate to say the remaking of our hearts is beyond our comprehension. God, our Creator, is more intimately aware of who we are and what we need than we have any hope of understanding. Therefore, this change He is able to bring about in us is the single most important and complete change we can experience.

It is a complete heart transplant; not in a physical sense, but in a spiritual, emotional, and moral sense. It's an emptying out and cleansing of the storeroom of our hearts.

This single verse lists a number of ways God recreates the individual and the group when this heart transplant is accomplished. Let's explore some of those changes we experience by pulling them out phrase by phrase.

God says He will give this group of people "one heart." This phrasing is colloquial. The people going through this transformation will share a unity of purpose and intention with other people going through the same renovations. This is important because the nature of humanity is that we are social creatures. Even though God might be taking us on a trip that is uniquely ours, we will do better if we know we're not alone in our priorities and commitments. Therefore, God almost always gives us a group, a collection of others who can relate to our heart choices and commitments. In the passage in Ezekiel, the group was the nation of Israel. For Peter, the group was the other apostles. For us, the group is a Bible-believing church. Satan tries hard to keep us away from this God-designed support group. He will try to convince us they are not helpful, not spiritual, and unnecessary. Don't believe the devil; we need the church.

In the second key phrase, God would give us "a new spirit." It would be easy to believe this refers to the way the Holy Spirit is at work in the New Testament believer. New designates this spirit works in a way the Old Testament had not experienced. This could be the meaning of the passage, but also take into consideration the possibility that it's a matter of rearranging the attitude of our lives. The new spirit has to do with a peace, joy, and whole new set of reactions to the world around us. We are no longer hardwired to react in the same ways we always have. An internal attitude gives birth to an external reaction. If the attitude is bad, the reaction will be bad, and, the final result will be bad. We nip the process in the bud by letting God give us a new attitude.

Next it says, "I will remove their heart of stone from their bodies and give them a heart of flesh." This is the center of the heart transplant I mentioned earlier. I believe what is described here as a heart of stone is a heart where it stored up evil until its very nature changed. The cumulative effect of all this evil was the heart became hard, like rock. Oddly enough, many people in today's world would see this as a positive thing, since the heart of stone cannot be broken and cannot be affected any more by the hurts of life. However, it isn't a good thing. It's a horrible tragedy. We were created to have a heart of flesh. A heart of flesh can store positive moral attributes and draw from those to become a person of astounding accomplishments. God created us with great potential.

There is a sense in which the change is made all at once, done in an instant transformation. It isn't described as a gradual, life-long process but as a single, life-changing event. This is part of the problem with so many philosophies of life; they are looking for what is humanly possible in a lifetime. Far greater is what is divinely possible in an instant. From this point on, the individual human's story moves forward. If this individual life has been converted by God in this manner, the human life growing out of the event is a partnership. It's a lifetime of building the new heart in better and stronger ways, a journey undertaken by the human, but chosen and guided by God. Don't miss the all-important starting point. It begins as an act of God giving us the new heart. It begins with a moment's decision we make to allow God to undertake a heart transplant.

Notice the reason why God makes this change in individuals. "…so they may follow My statutes, keep My ordinances, and practice them." These changes are made so we'll have the ability to follow God's laws. In other words, this change of heart allows us to begin to live right. Prior to this change, we were enslaved by the storehouse full of sin we'd accumulated over our lifetime. Our hearts where full of this sin and constantly caused us to continue in it. After the heart transplant, past patterns of sin no longer dictate our choices. Paul describes similar events in the New Testament when he says we are enslaved by sin, but in Christ we can be set free from sin. The weight of those past decisions is no longer stored up inside us. God has set us free from our history, from our storehouse of evil, and from the hearts we earned with our past bad choices.

"Then they will be My people, and I will be their God." This verse speaks of a relationship between these people and God after this transition occurs. God is always God. He judges all of humanity whether they believe in Him or not, accept or reject Him. Be certain we understand this fact; our faith, our actions, and our decisions will not change facts. God is Boss, and this simple truth is a fact we must embrace. This passage uses two possessive pronouns—my and their—to describe a relationship based on more than facts. Making a decision to allow God to change our hearts can only take place if we determine He is the rightful ruler of our lives. If we make this decision, then we submit to Him in such a way our relationship is not only dictated by facts but is one of choice.

The choice to allow God to be our God is predicated by two criteria. First, we have to understand and admit we can't run our lives appropriately. We do not know what is best. We did not create ourselves, and we do not exist for our own purposes. God created humanity. We exist for His purposes. Everything we did previously, everything we filled our hearts with, was wrong. This admission of our own failure, this admission of our own sin, is essential to allowing God to give us a heart transplant.

The second criteria for accepting God as personally ours, is submission. It's possible for us to admit our way is wrong and God's way is right but still not be willing to turn from doing things our own way. The decision for God to be Lord of our life isn't complete until we are ready to go all the way and commit ourselves to live under His command. Admission is a key step to bringing about change, but sometimes people make admissions as a sad realization they are headed in the wrong direction. Until they redirect themselves, nothing changes. The decision to allow God to be Lord of our life is not complete until we decide we will trust Him to lead us and we will do your best to follow His lead. This turning away from our way and committing ourselves to do our best to follow His way is the biblical concept of repentance.

The decision to follow God isn't complete until we decide we trust Him. When things get complicated, we must follow what we know to be God's will rather than fixing things with a sinful human solution. Think about a newly married couple. They have decided to trust one another, but sometime in the first year one or both of them will be tempted to quit and run for home. In this moment of temptation, the marriage may appear to be falling apart. If they stay and work on it, they will forge a stronger bond. Similar decisions face us when determining to trust God with our lives. Stick with God, and we will find Him trustworthy.

We must also do our best to follow God's will. This means we consider what God says is right and wrong with every decision. We choose not to live on auto-pilot; we allow God to lead us. In order to do this, we need to be aware of Scripture. Therefore, we must study it closely. Too many people claim to follow God but refuse to put out the effort to become familiar enough with God's Word to stay on track. With time, we will also be able to discern how God speaks to us individually in order to lead us in specific aspects of life.

A very central part of having this heart surgery is to make a personal commitment to let God be our God. Too often, people step through a ceremony like the sinner's prayer or a baptism and expect they now have the whole God thing under control. Nothing could be further from the truth. If they never actually made a commitment to Him or intended to change the way they live, then they are still wildly out of control. If we think this is a decision we already made in our lives, let's think it through once again and be sure of where we stand.

This discussion went the long way around the barn to talk about a salvation commitment. The gospel will never change, but it was important for us to talk about this decision in a new way. If we approach it as we always have, then the typical response will be to skim over it without giving it full consideration. By approaching it in a new way, I hope to persuade us to go back and reconsider our salvation decisions from their very foundation.

This is the single most important event of our lives and our eternities, but it is also the best starting place for strong hearts. A person who is wholly surrendered to God has the single greatest tool for unleashing the power of their heart, specifically the heart of flesh God has put in them. By living in right relationship with God through Christ, He guides us in how to guard our heart and what to store up in it as we move forward from this point.

It will take some critical steps for us to turn our lives over to Christ in this way.

First, we have to admit and realize who we are now isn't working. If we're still holding out hope that the way we've shaped our hearts without His help is good enough, then we're not ready to trust Him. If we are willing to admit our situation is hopeless, our way is worthless, and it must be left behind in order to follow God's path, then we've taken a first step. Romans 3:23 says, "For all have sinned and fall short of the glory of God." This verse reiterates one of our foundational lessons about heart. Everyone has a heart filled with the wrong things; it's beyond our ability to prevent this apart from God.

But in God, through Christ, we have an ability to change this, an ability to start over. We can allow Jesus to provide a new heart in the experience described in Ezekiel 11:18-21. The point of the cross was for Jesus to make a difference in our lives, one we were incapable of making for ourselves. The cross represents Jesus, God the Son, proving how much He loves us. This love reached out to us to allow us the choice to give Him permission to remake us in this way. He doesn't make this change of heart in us without our desiring and inviting Him to do so. Through the cross, He woos us, draws us to Him so we can know we made the right decision. Romans 5:6 says, "For while we were still helpless, at the appointed moment, Christ died for the ungodly." A couple of verses later, Romans 5:8 says, "But God proves His own love for us in that while we were still sinners Christ died for us!" The cross, in one sense, demonstrates God going to great lengths to get our attention with a great act of sacrificial love. After He has our attention, He offers us the greatest gift we could ever receive. God offers us forgiveness of sins and a brand new heart to start over with.

In another sense, Christ died on the cross to provide the perfect, once-for-all sacrifice for sin in His own body. His own sinlessness and Deity made Him the perfect sacrifice, so our entire lifetime of wrong choices could be forgiven all at once. When we allow Christ to give us this new heart, the sin in our life is forgiven. God uses sacrifice, the shedding of blood, to demonstrate visibly how serious our wrongdoing is. His self-sacrifice on the cross was a great demonstration of love, but it also demonstrated God does not and should not take our sin lightly. Neither should we. Hebrews 9:22 says, "According to the law almost everything is purified with blood, and without the shedding of blood there is no forgiveness."

In Christ and His self-sacrifice on the cross, we have a God-given opportunity to be made new in a remarkable way. He offers to give us forgiveness for our mistakes—not just past mistakes, but future ones as well. We are given a new heart that isn't weighed down by our history of storing up evil but is now ready to be filled anew with better choices.

The next question becomes how an individual allows God to make this change in them. The answer is permission and submission. We mentioned earlier Jesus will not come and make changes in our lives unless we are a willing participant. We signal our willingness to Him by believing His ability to accomplish this change and by going to Him and voicing our desire for Him to take this action. Romans 10:8b-13 says, "This is the message of faith that we proclaim: if you confess with your mouth, 'Jesus is Lord,' and believe in your heart that God raised Him from the dead, you will be saved. With the heart one believes, resulting in righteousness, and with the mouth one confesses, resulting in salvation. Now the Scripture says, No one who believes on Him will be put to shame, for there is no distinction between Jew and Greek, since the same Lord of all is rich to all who call on Him. For everyone who calls on the name of the Lord will be saved."

Notice the phrasing, "believe in your heart." Remember what we have learned about heart. It's whatever we choose to make the center of our personality and our existence. By putting Christ into the storeroom of the heart first, we are accepting the truth that He is the Son of God and the rightful ruler of our lives. If we accept this truth, the only sane response is to make Him the center of how we live. If He is the center of how we live, then we have changed our course from living for ourselves to living His way. My favorite way of saying it is we make Him Boss.

Looking back at Romans 10:9-10, let's also talk about "confess with your mouth." This phrasing means we need to tell Jesus we want this change to take place. Part of becoming a new creation in Christ is to ask Him for it. Another part of confessing with our mouths is being honest with others, telling them Christ has become the center of our lives. A person who has changed their whole pattern of living will not keep this news to themselves.

Undoubtedly, many people believe they've already made this decision. Just as certainly, some portion of us did not make a valid decision. This possibility is why Philippians 2:12 says, "So then, my dear friends, just as you have always obeyed, not only in my presence, but now even more in my absence, work out your own salvation with fear and trembling." Without meaning to sow doubts, every follower of Christ must be willing to reconsider our salvation. If we don't remember it, then a pattern-changing event never took place. If we didn't intend to change our patterns and only wanted to secure a place in heaven, then we didn't get a new heart. If either of these possibilities describes us, then we need to make the decision afresh. Make the decision right now, even if it might be a repeat of a past decision. It's important to be certain we are not misleading ourselves.

If we know or suspect we've never made this decision, then we should do two things. First, pray the prayer listed below or one like it and let Jesus know we want His salvation and forgiveness. Second, we must look closely at our lives and be ready to make a lot of changes that will emphasize and empower our decision to redirect our lives from our patterns to His patterns. Go big in repentance. Tell everyone. Be ready and willing to learn about serving God. To do this, we need to find a good Bible-believing church. I recommend a Southern Baptist church, but if this is not available, let God lead us to a church that knows and teaches what it means to completely change the patterns of our lives through the power of the cross.

Here is a sample prayer to turn our lives over to Jesus. Remember, the exact wording isn't as important as the humble willingness to turn our lives over to Christ and the intent of our hearts to live fully in this new pattern.

Dear Jesus, I want my entire life to be changed by Your power. I know my way has been accumulating sin in my heart. I admit I've been wrong, and I ask for Your forgiveness. I confess You as Lord and ask You to be the rightful Ruler in my heart and Boss of my life. Give me a whole new heart and let me start over living for You. Thank You for saving me. Lord, please give me the boldness to tell everyone about this change. In Jesus name, amen.

If you've made this decision for the first time or, for that matter, if you're certain you've made it in the past, congratulations! It's the most important decision. Not just of your lifetime, but of eternity.

Chapter 11

The accumulation of courage

We have defined heart as a storeroom and spoken of three things stored there deserving of special consideration: self-image, morality, and courage. Courage is one of the most important stores in our heart, and we need the ability to control it. It is necessary to realize courage is a learned behavior. Learned behaviors are reinforced the more they are practiced and can be lost if they are not practiced. Because of this, it's not just a matter of whether one has courage, but it's also important to think about exercising courage. To put it another way, how well courage is reinforced in the individual is just as important as finding it present.

My church had a Men's Desert Day. In order to participate in this event, my son and I borrowed two quads from a friend. Because we don't have a toy hauler, we rode the ATVs to the event, which was about ten miles across the desert. When we first left the quad owner's home, we drove with white-knuckled caution. Shortly, we came across our first hill. It was a mild rise on hard packed sand, but we both stopped and looked at it like it was Mount Everest. In fact, we had some mild difficulty getting over this first rise.

By the time we got to the event, we cruised over hills four times as high and a lot steeper. Our speed was no longer limited to single digits. Far from the white knuckles experienced in the first few minutes, we settled down and relaxed. Instead of the stressful experience it started out as, riding became a whole lot of fun.

What changed? We accumulated courage. Each hill we conquered was a victory that allowed us to attempt something bigger. Even the failures gave us experience. They taught us what not to do. Since victory followed every defeat, based on the new skills we were learning, even these failures ultimately added to our confidence. This is a simple example of what it means to accumulate courage. This may not appear so much a gathering of courage as it does simply getting use to the machines. Getting used to a device is, in essence, acquiring the skills and confidence necessary to operate it. The confidence portion of this equation is the end result of accumulating courage.

In this example, confidence is the courage to use the devices without expecting to break them, get hurt, or have some other disastrous outcome. When courage lacks, fear reigns. When we allow courage to displace fear, the ability to set aside fear becomes a form of habit. Courage looks at a situation with positive expectations and hope, while discouragement puts our eyes on every opportunity as a calamity waiting to happen.

We can see the same process at work in team sports. At the beginning of the high school football season, the players are somewhat reserved in their hits. They have some underlying fears both about getting hurt and hurting someone else. With time and good coaching, they accumulate courage. Their hits in the latter part of the season make those early attempts look like child's play. In an important sense, they were. They "played" with their ability until they gained enough confidence and experience to put their full potential and skill into the game. When they stopped "playing," their hits on the field became purposeful, aimed at accomplishing the goals of the game.

Courage is cumulative. These are small examples. The human experience goes well beyond games and recreation. If we are to understand courage, we need to discuss it and utilize it in the weightier matters of life.

There is no doubt that the men and women who shaped our nation and our world did so by mastering courage. Individuals like George Washington leading the revolutionary soldiers across the Potomac, Thomas Edison enduring thousands of failures in his attempt to make a light bulb, and Susan B. Anthony campaigning for suffrage did so by using their courage to move forward against impossible odds. These individuals were capable of making such momentous differences in this world because they had the necessary courage. Since they had formed the habit of being courageous, they were able to seize opportunities others would not have had the gumption to handle.

It may seem like a long journey from learning to ride an ATV to accomplishing world-changing triumphs. We must understand that greater accomplishments are enabled by consistently and faithfully acting with appropriate courage in the smaller things. If God leads us to ride a quad, learning to do so may be a necessary step to changing the world. It may be one of hundreds or thousands of times when God gives us the opportunity to respond with either faithful courage or faithless cowardice. A person who is going to be capable of valorously moving forward in an issue of world-changing importance must have a foundation of smaller courageous decisions already laid.

We should not expect a short pattern to yield massive rewards. We are spoiled and no longer expect to work for our achievements. We expect we can be people of world-class character or world-shaking achievement in a few easy steps or by spending a few minutes each day. What has always been true is still true. The things most valuable require the most serious and consistent effort. We cannot expect a short-lived foray out of fear and into courage will make us a courageous person forever. We should strive for the huge rewards but do so understanding the return will not be quick. In fact, quick returns work against us in the long run.

We also need to be careful not to compartmentalize courage. It is natural to look at ourselves and think we are a person of courage. Most anybody can find some activity in their life where they express courage on a regular basis. Compartmentalizing courage into these few areas of life is not what we need to do. Strive to practice courage in all areas of life, at all times and in all ways. Make courageous living a lifetime pattern.

Someone who shows courage in part of their life, but not in all of life, may be gaining nothing from the displayed courage. Extreme sports are very popular in our society. The people who practice great courage in these pursuits may do so as a salve to cover the hurts from a lack of courage in other, less frivolous arenas of accomplishment. These other pursuits would mean more to them, but they carry more risk. The adventurer fails to muster the courage to face those risks. I'm not saying the risks they fail to take are risks of physical harm, like those faced in extreme sports. The risks I refer to may be in the arena of business, social embarrassment, or academic achievement.

The world is full of men who fail to express courage in the workplace because the fear of failure overcomes their daring. After all, a man knows supporting his family is a primary responsibility. Therefore, the decision to avoid stepping out and start a new business may be very sensible. Most new businesses fail, and if this happens, he knows he won't be supporting his family in the manner they are accustomed to. (We certainly don't want to encourage anyone to abandon their financial responsibility toward their family.) But, not taking those risks builds a pattern in the heart. If we step back because it would be a foolish move, then it's wise to back off. If we step back from a good opportunity out of nothing but fear, then it's a heart-bending moment.

Everyone knows being in a long term relationship means making commitments to another person. Those commitments include a degree of self-sacrifice that may seem difficult to undertake voluntarily. It doesn't take a lot of research to realize many people, if not most, change afterward—and not always for the better. So many people will simply not make a long-term commitment. This decision is to choose cowardice instead of courage.

Many people end their educational journey, not because they have adequate training for everything they desire to accomplish in the workplace, but because they begin to see themselves as unable to excel in those academic circles. Instead of moving forward in the face of this risk, they stop their training and adjust their life to these limitations. Instead of allowing education to be a tool in their hands whereby they shape what they become, their fear of failure becomes the limiter of what they can be.

Many people fail to be strong hearted because they don't allow courage to extend into all areas of their life. These same people might well project the strongest of all demeanors to the world around them. They might be the bravest of hunters. They might throw themselves across the racetrack at breakneck speed. They might be the boldest street fighters in town. These activities might be the way they convince themselves they are not living in cowardice. They cover for their disappointments in themselves based on their own lack of accomplishment or failure to risk.

Don't misunderstand. I'm not saying every person involved in bold activities is a coward inside. As I said earlier, bold activities might be part of a larger pattern of courage in our lives. Take this as a strong warning, though; we must not consider ourselves a person of courage unless our courage extends into our entire life. It's not enough to live strong only in recreation and hobbies. We must also live with courage personally, professionally, and spiritually. While these three areas occur to me as the major arenas of consequence, there are other arenas that could be of importance, depending on whom we are and where God is leading us.

Think about the connection between courage and adventure. Everyone I know has a sense of adventure. It's stronger in some people than in others, but everyone has it. In some people it's aimed differently. Different activities strike them as the type of adventure they want to be involved in. Some live it out in academic circles, while others express it in social exchanges. For others, it may be team sports, while some prefer the isolation of the wild outdoors.

We cannot live the same adventures over and over again and be satisfied with them. Parts of what make an activity into an adventure are the challenges and hardships we face and overcome. We should live life as an adventure, looking for new experiences and new activities. Within these new endeavors, we find new victories and achievements. This type of attitude about life assists us greatly in accumulating courage and building strength into our hearts. While we are not to express our sense of adventure in ways that are more likely to end up in injury than victory, I would encourage us to go out and find some area where we can explore and overcome new challenges.

This sense of adventure is useful in providing us a proving ground for courage. Remember what I said earlier: courage in recreational pursuits cannot become the only part of our life where courage is expressed. When a person adds recreational pursuits to a life already boldly lived, it can be a useful way of further building their hearts. There is a real connection between accumulating courage and living with an adventurous spirit.

I believe life should be lived adventurously and none so much as the life lived for Christ. Living for Jesus is the greatest adventure. The adversities we need to overcome are our own selfish desires. The victories to be achieved are eternal. No road can be as spectacular as the one lived under God's direction. Living for Jesus is the greatest adventure. If we know Jesus Christ as Savior, then all we have to do for our life to be a wonderful adventure is set aside our own desires, agendas, plans, and purposes and to begin living fully for Him instead. He will take us places and work through us in ways we never imagined.

Living under God's direction has caused me to see places on this earth I don't believe I ever would have visited charting my own course. Among my fondest memories are standing on a sheer rock face in Norway that dropped several thousand feet down into a fiord. I made the hike with a youth group while volunteering for an English-speaking church in Stavanger, Norway. Another favorite is playing paintball with a group of young adults and friends from church. I sweat and panted for air under the protective mask, not so much from physical activity as from the addictive mix of positive and negative adrenaline. Positive adrenaline from the thought I was going to get somebody, and negative adrenaline with the thought someone was going to get me. Another adventure was on a rock climbing trip with a group of teenagers. Although not in the best of shape, I made it to the top of an intermediate climb. I believe the Christian life should be an adventure, and I defy anyone who expects being a believer means ruining our fun.

Courage is cumulative, and by accumulating courage through facing greater and greater challenges, we train ourselves to face life courageously. Living life as a process of courageous and appropriate adventures builds strength into our hearts. Courage must be a full life pattern and not limited to safer areas of achievement.

Society presses men to shape their adventurous spirit in all the wrong ways. While writing this, I sit in an auto shop waiting for them to finish working on my car. Workers in the next room are talking about how drunk they were the night before.

Getting drunk is one of many examples of different activities our society uses as an outlet for adventure. Let's be wiser than this. Although it does seemingly fit the model in some ways, becoming intoxicated is not expressing a sense of adventure. It's giving one's self over to a false sense of adventure. Alcohol lowers our inhibitions, so the actions taken under its influence are not courageous. The sense of exhilaration is not real, but a chemically induced lie.

In relationship to our heart, seeking adventure in immoral activities always undermines our heart's strength. Instead of accumulating courage to achieve and do good things, we reinforce negative patterns.

We can accumulate courage to build our hearts and make our lives bolder, stronger, and better. Be careful though, because pursuing courage by sinning only makes us more likely to sin again. The pattern of sin grows and makes our lives increasingly worse. Many men seek adventure by charming women into promiscuous compromises. This is just another example of an adventure that tears us and others down instead of building us up. Other examples of false adventures include physical risks out of sync with any possible accomplishment or benefit, breaking laws for the thrill of it, and manipulating people for the sense of power it gives us.

The sense of adventure can be a great part of life, but it must be lived out under submission to Christ. It will not build a stronger heart unless the activity is morally positive.

Chapter 12

BUSTING OUT BIG

The heart is a storehouse of the good and bad things in our lives, which allows either good or bad things to overflow into our behaviors. Unfortunately, we live in a fallen world, and the world force feeds us a steady stream of pollution. These negative behaviors spill back out in our own choices and actions, even when we try to avoid them. After falling into the same negative action a few times, it becomes a habit for us. How do we change these negative tendencies?

Repentance is a matter of changing patterns. Repentance is a total change of behavior; it is turning from doing things our way to doing things God's way. In this manner, repentance is a matter of completely changing our patterns and habits.

If we don't produce a change in our patterns, we haven't changed anything at all. We haven't changed what we're storing up in our hearts or our availability to be used by God in powerful ways. Therefore, I want to spend some time talking specifically about repentance. I like to call it pattern busting.

Unfortunately, our churches are full of people who live in the exact same patterns they did prior to salvation. People live exactly like the world around them and somehow believe they are different. They delude themselves with their different attitude toward negative behaviors, their adopted new goals, and their improved priorities. These internal changes may convince them they've changed, but their external actions haven't followed suit. The habits might never change if they are not intentional in repenting.

One of the basic tools for making external changes is to follow the examples of others. On several occasions, Paul mentions in his epistles that the new believers should follow the patterns of his example. Positive examples are precious. When there are good examples we can emulate, learning the behaviors and patterns of Christian living is easier. Similarly, in times of war, combatants are told they should take any opportunity to kill an enemy commander. The simple reason for this strategy is that it's hard to train recruits in the art of warfare; it is far easier to say, "Men, follow me." It is far easier for a new believer to tag along with a mature believer to learn how to witness, tithe, study the Bible, pray, and work with other believers.

I notice we have a multitude of classes to train each other how to do these things within our churches, but the Bible establishes a model of apprenticeship more often than it does a classroom education. I would not assert this latter model is completely absent from the biblical examples, but a more personal, one-to-one technique was employed more often. Jesus picked a small group of disciples and taught them. He even had a select group within the disciples he spent extra time with. Paul put extra time and energy into certain leaders in order to train them in ministry and leadership, such as Timothy and Onesimus. Both of these examples can be countered by times they taught large groups, but the small group teaching still held greater oomph.

This can be difficult in today's churches, because we lack good examples. To make matters worse, the worst examples tend to rule the day. Hanging out in churches all these years I have heard a negative attitude toward new believers. Church members say a new believer's excitement and desire to change is temporary. The existing believers often feel the sooner they get over it, the better. The biblical reality is we're not supposed get over conversion. Pushing a new believer to return back to "normal" patterns is equivalent to asking them to live the Christian life without repentance. Telling a new believer to stop being so different is a lot like telling them to stop listening to God.

Of course, there are times a new believer goes overboard and tries to set the whole world right in ten minutes. I believe more often, conflicts between new believers and other believers happen because the new believers remind the other believers of areas they haven't fully surrendered to God or failed to mature. Truly mature believers are not in these conflicts with new believers.

Another reason churches are full of half-repentant Christians is we have a temptation to soft sell repentance. We have such a strong desire to see people saved we take the hard ingredients of salvation out of our presentations. We can describe the process in terms that leave repentance out of the formula. This is disastrous. It is false teaching and something we preachers will be held accountable for when we stand before Christ. Despite the fact I know this—and have known it for a long time—I still catch myself wanting to see decisions and trying to make the process easier for people. We would never state it so obviously as this, but sometimes the call to salvation comes out like this: "Come forward now and pray with me. We can work on whether or not you really mean it later."

We soft sell repentance by not mentioning it in our gospel presentations. We tell people they have to A – admit they are a sinner, B – believe Jesus is God's son, and C – Confess Jesus as their Savior and Lord. When we say it like this, we know exactly what it means to say Jesus is Lord of our life. It means He is given total control of our life. When Jesus is Boss, He will lead us away from sin. This implies repentance. Repentance is also implied in the admission of our sin. If we believe our behavior is wrong, we will want to change it. In other words, the concept of repentance is hidden within the phrasing of the presentation. The problem is the people hearing the message often have no clue it's in there.

Many have bought into the false idea being saved by grace means repentance is an unnecessary construct. They have a hard time with repentance, because they see it as a work. We are saved by grace and not by works. Therefore, if repentance is a work we do in order to be saved, then it is not compatible with being saved by grace. This is a false understanding based on an incorrect doctrine of salvation.

Salvation is a relationship with God. Since God is not like a human in many significant ways, our relationship with Him is different than our relationships with each other. Any relationship with Him that asks Him to deny His nature would be insincere. In order to have a relationship with God, we must be willing to admit He is rightfully the Boss. Further, we want Him to be in control, because we know things work better when He is. Salvation is a matter of choosing repentance by coming to the conclusion God's way is better than ours, and our way will always have sin at its root.

When someone comes to God for salvation, He sees within them their true intentions. The person who wants to honor Him and allow Him to be their God, in both their words and their patterns, will be saved. In others, He sees other intentions at work. It may be a desire to avoid hell, to be a better person, or any number of other motives that fall short of the desire to let God be God, and specifically, their Lord.

In order to be saved, repentance has to be part of our intention. The completion of repentance is taken later as a response to salvation. It is a follow-through by the person who has already been saved. It isn't done to earn salvation. The real work of repentance is done as a response to salvation. Repentance is following through with a part of our commitment made to God when we were saved. Pattern busting, or repentance, must be part of what we are willing to do for Jesus. If we are not willing to change our lives and our priorities, then we never admitted our way was wrong and His way is right.

Most of us operate on autopilot in regard to our priorities. We don't consciously consider them as we meander through life's decisions, big and small. Instead, we rely on the moment to dictate what decision we make. This approach might work if our priorities are in order, but too often, the squeaky wheel gets the grease. We are all guilty of this. We temporarily bump something in our life to a higher priority. We hope this compromise will give us peace from the nagging item and let us do the other things we deem more important.

This becomes a problem, because it allows the devil to make us so busy with unimportant, lower priorities, and we never address the real issues of life. When we live on autopilot, we run from fire to fire. Since the devil can control the fires, in essence he gets to control us by setting the fires strategically in opposition to our supposed priorities. Even when our priorities are in order, it's necessary to keep the autopilot turned off and to consciously decide what is most important for us to address from moment to moment.

For Christians, the proper set of priorities looks something like this: (1) God, (2) spouse, (3) kids, and (4) employment. Each one may draw their list a little differently than I do, but if we don't have God at the top, we need to get Him there. It is important to keep God at the top of the list, because He will balance all the other areas for us. We must be willing to rearrange the order of priorities. Make God the top priority, and then let Him order the rest.

Next, think like a skater. Skaters may act and think in ways we shouldn't emulate, but they have one trait I encourage us to borrow. When it comes to all good things in life, particularly in regards to repentance, go big or go home. Let me say this in another way: when it comes to changing patterns, go for overkill. Sometimes it's best to be ridiculous so we remember things are different now.

When it comes to pattern busting—go big. One man decided a lot of television programming was unhealthy, so he had the cable disconnected. If he is ever tempted to watch television, he can't. There's probably some healthy content he's missing out on, but by going big he made sure the unhealthy content never reaches his mind. If he desires entertainment, he watches videos, which can be carefully screened and chosen. His decision to completely cut off the cable reminds and empowers him to use discernment in other areas of life as well.

Was this foolishness or great wisdom? Was this a decision lived out in relationship with Christ, or does this action make the gentleman some kind of lunatic? How we answer reveals whether we are willing to go big. Our willingness to go big or not reveals whether Christ is treasured in our heart above all these other things. So go big or go home.

How can we go big? We should be willing to change our appearance. I'm not saying we need to look a certain way to be a believer. But, sometimes looking a certain way is associated with our way of living prior to becoming a Christian. In some instances, our appearance can be a stumbling block for other believers. Be willing to go big in regards to how we look both for our own sake and for the sake of fellowship.

There can be a multitude of aspects to how our appearance needs to change in order to empower pattern busting in our lives. A lot of people I know have T-shirt collections. The messages on T-shirts can be filled with negative content that fills our hearts with evil. Most often this is in the form of written words, but it can also include things like product endorsements, racy pictures, and violent images. If our intent is to live for Christ, then perhaps all these need to hit the trash barrel. If it seems like too much to ask, maybe we haven't turned our whole life over to Christ. It may be we love a certain look more than we love Jesus. The suggestion the two are not compatible is threatening, because it reveals this falsehood.

For many women in today's world, pattern busting means they will want to change the way they dress. The little black dress considered a wardrobe standard has more leg showing than is edifying for men. Going big would mean not wearing it and not being a stumbling block to those men. The same would be true for low-rise jeans, bare midriffs, tight sweaters, and a number of other fashions. Before we reject this as unrealistic, the question is, are we willing to go big in pattern busting? I believe this is good advice for women and girls of all ages. For some it's essential, because the way they dress has brought about the negative interactions with men from their old pattern. They desire to be different and need to change this in order to bust this negative pattern.

We may also need to change our haircut. Several examples come to mind, but the first one that jumps out at me is from little pockets of people in our community known as skinheads. Occasionally violent, sometimes racist groups sport buzz cuts. If anyone has a history with these groups and wants to change a pattern, they might be wise to let their hair grow out to more common lengths. For others, it might be the opposite. Perhaps long hair or a Mohawk was a symbol of defiance in their life. If they are serious about pattern busting, they should go beyond the norm in making changes that reflect a new heart.

These changes are not gender specific. Men may need to watch their choice of clothing, and women might need to change their hair. If we want to live a different life, then we need to send a different signal. Although God looks at the heart, the people around us look at our external. More importantly, we see our own external every time we look in the mirror. If something about our style reminds us of the wrong attitudes and patterns, it's only common sense to change it.

Another area of concern is body art. I find it to be anything but aesthetic. But whether we think positively or negatively about piercings and tattoos, we should take an honest look at what it is and consider whether or not it needs to be changed in order to reflect our new pattern. In some cases, we may need to let piercings heal over. In other cases, someone will decide to cover tattoos. The choice may be something as simple as wearing long sleeves. Others might have new tattoos added over the old to make them more acceptable. One person I know went back and had clothes added to the girls in his existing tattoos. Other people may even choose to have them surgically removed. Please don't think of any of this as silly. Make a conscious decision how to handle it in your individual case. The question remains: are we willing to do whatever it takes? Go big or go home. If anything on earth is too much for Christ to ask of us, then He isn't number one in our life.

Entertainment is another prominent area for us to deal with. If we want to change the patterns of our life, then be willing to go big in regards to our music, movies, video games, and internet usage. Many people would find themselves spiritually stronger if they deleted all their online profiles. Other people need to realize their recreation, even if the activity itself is not overtly wrong, can be a factor swallowing their time and therefore controlling their priorities.

Two areas of concern when it comes to entertainment are our ears and eyes. A number of people have noted our ears and eyes are like gates that allow positive or negative input to invade our brains and, therefore, our hearts. We need to be realistic and admit the primary source of the heart-shaping onslaught in these two areas comes from entertainment. If we watch movies, read magazines, and play games containing suggestive or sexual content, it's an obvious problem and needs to be changed. A simple decision to go big in changing this content, even if it seems like overkill, saves us from a lot of problems down the line.

The other area of concern is our ears. In college, I received a challenge to review the lyrics on my record collection. I did so, and I broke several records and threw them away. In order to make a strong statement, I burned some of them. Looking back on it, I should have disposed of more than I did at the time. A part of the significance of this event in my life was the number of people who were upset with me. Several students said I shouldn't have destroyed those albums. Instead they felt I should have given them away or sold them for a few bucks. I made the decision they were unhealthy and subjecting someone else to those words and ideas would have been wrong. I could have made a few dollars. I could have justified it by saying the records were already available in any used record store. I made a choice to bust a pattern instead. Selling the records wouldn't signal as serious a change as destroying them did. Go big or go home.

Social habits are another important area of change. Where we go for our down time and our social gatherings might need to change in order to bust the patterns in our life. For some people it may be important to change their existing circle of friends. Don't assume this is extreme. Many people in our society have their friendships centered on un-Christian activities such as drinking, drugs, or promiscuity. These friendships may be genuine, but since we cannot be around them without being around the pattern we are trying to escape, we need to change our friends. Be willing to go for overkill to escape the life patterns trying to kill us. I was recently in a class taught by a drug abuse counselor. He stated that a user who refuses to change his patterns of who, what, and where will never stop being a user. This is true for other sins as well. If we're having problems busting our patterns, it may be caused by stubbornly hanging on to things around the pattern that are not actually wrong. But, these side issues empower the negative habits we want to leave behind.

Pattern busting is a whole lot of work. However, it's the kind of work that rewards us over and over again. A person who is successful in pattern busting finds it to be the most liberating and empowering aspect of their walk with Christ. This is no surprise. Scripture defines our sin as enslaving us. The pattern holds us in its power, under its control. We experience great freedom in Christ when we are able to step away from its domination. The strength the pattern sapped is now given back to us. As an unexpected perk, we are also given the liberty to accomplish greater things. Pattern busting isn't easy, but the go big mentality makes it easier. This idea of going for overkill is also likely to multiply the rewards of our pattern busting and our accomplishments.

Go big or go home. Be willing to go for overkill. Too many Christians are afraid of looking like spiritual lunatics. I think the devil has convinced us to be afraid of fundamentalists and fanatics. In reality, we stop short of accomplishing the basic steps of Christian growth out of our fear of the extremes. Somewhere in my life I decided it would be better to risk being a fanatic than to be relegated to the irrelevant majority most Christians have unconsciously populated. In some ways I may go too far, but I honestly doubt I've even begun to go far enough.

I had a preaching professor in seminary who commented about inflection in the voice when speaking in public. He said when the speaker thinks they have gone too far, they have barely begun to go far enough. I suspect the same is true of living for Jesus. How could we ever go too far? When we feel like we are going too far, we are just beginning.

Chapter 13

THE DEVIL'S PLAYGROUND

Every year the Pikes Peak Hill Climb is held outside of Colorado Springs. It's a race against the clock as different drivers start at the bottom of the mountain, at about 6,000 feet in elevation, and charge to the top of the 14,110 feet peak. About two-thirds of the way up is a spot called Devil's Playground. It's a favorite spot for people to watch the hill climb. They drive up the night before, set up camp, and wake up early the next morning in anticipation of the roar of race cars.

Woe unto anyone who sleepwalks. Devil's Playground is a flat spot on the side of the mountain. On three sides, it drops precipitously down for thousands of feet. People choose this spot because it has a clear view over the portion of the course where the race cars achieve their highest speeds. The high speeds are possible here because of a long, straight stretch leading up to this point. At Devil's Playground, there's a switchback where the cars must slow down in order to make a 180 degree turn before continuing up the course. Roaring toward this switchback, the race cars can achieve speeds up to 140 miles per hour. This straight stretch also happens to be aimed straight at the dangerous drop-off surrounding Devil's Playground.

The spectators at Devil's Playground pick this spot because they want to see a driver miss the turn. Miss it wide enough and the race car launches out into space before succumbing to the force of gravity and plunging to a spectacular and deadly crash. They would agree this would be a terrible tragedy, but many spectators would also agree if it happened, they'd like to be there to see it.

I haven't looked it up, but I would be willing to bet more spectators than drivers have gone off the edge of Devil's Playground. They weren't there to take any kind of risk. They were there to watch someone else take the risk. But, by being in the vicinity of the edge, they were taking the risk, too. The dangers never entered their mind. They were so distracted by the activities of others they didn't realize they, too, were in danger.

Here is a foolishness many Christians participate in. They know right where the line is between right and wrong, and they purposely stay as close to it as possible. All the while they tell themselves they are doing nothing wrong, since they are on the correct side of the line. Their fascination with being as close as possible to the line reveals there is something already going wrong in their heart.

Time and time again the person who shouts loudest about how horrible a sin is turns out to be the person who falls hardest into the sin. They may be so fascinated by the sin they allow themselves to get unusually close to it. Then, they fall into it. Here is the lesson from Devil's Playground. When we stand on the edge, it takes a whole lot less of a nudge to knock us over.

This principle is again somewhat simple, somewhat obvious, but empowers us to avoid sin. Stay away from sin, not close to it. We must not in any way allow ourselves to enjoy watching it, thinking about it, or toying with it. Proverbs 23:17 says, "Don't be jealous of sinners; instead, always fear the LORD" This simple advice seems obvious to some and counterintuitive to others. It's good advice if we desire to keep our hearts clean.

Some Christians think of it as a mark of spiritual maturity to be as close to the line of sin as possible without going over. An example would be in regards to alcohol consumption. Some would be eager to point out the Bible does not command complete abstinence, but moderation. They have drawn the sin line at intoxication, and by drinking in moderation they believe they are flexing their spiritual discipline muscles by running right up to the line and stopping.

Complete abstinence from alcohol is wisdom, even though abstaining from all alcohol is a modern day construct rather than a biblical mandate. (Although, I think I can build a biblical case for not drinking, too.) Some

Christians drink and encourage others to have a drink every now and then, but prevent becoming intoxicated. Not surprising to anyone is the fact some percentage of those who start off drinking in moderation become alcoholics. They know some people who drink in moderation will lose control. They don't consider it might be them, personally, who fall into this trap. It never could have happened if they hadn't been in the devil's playground in the first place.

When we play as close as possible to the line of sin, it only takes a nudge to knock us over. It might seem progressive or logical to assert any activity on the correct side of the line of sin is okay. Since we serve God, we have an enemy who is always willing to supply us with a nudge in the wrong direction. Once we turn our lives over to Christ, this enemy knows he can do nothing to get us back into his family. His mission changes from keeping us out of God's family to making sure we aren't useful to God's purposes. When we stand as close to the line of sin as we can, we are cooperating with the devil in his goal of making us useless Christians.

Sometimes Christians tolerate being so close to the line of sin because they enjoy watching the sin. They get close to it because they vicariously experience the thrill of it by watching others as they participate in it. They believe they get the excitement of the sin without being tainted by it. This is not true.

It begins with watching others in the pattern. The sight may be repulsive, but for varying reasons, we keep watching. It may be because we don't want to be thought of as a wimp. Maybe it's because we wanted to talk about the latest sitcoms with co-workers. Or, maybe we were already prone to the activity in question. Whatever the reason, a key opportunity to remain pure was lost in the decision to keep watching.

Pretty soon it's not so much hideous as it's amusing, and from amusing it becomes provocative. Everything we see is stored up in the heart, and once enough of it is stored in this manner, participation is no longer abhorrent. Whatever is stored in the heart is going to come out again in behavior. Well-meaning Christians, who have every intention of staying on the correct side of the sin line, find themselves trapped in the most evil behaviors. It often started with a willingness to get as close to the sin line as possible. It's Lot all over again. At first, he lives in the same valley as

Sodom and Gomorrah, but in short order, he finds himself living in the center of town with trouble knocking on the door.

This is the principle of the devil's playground. Many people think the place where the devil has the most fun is down in the deepest, darkest pits of sin. I have come to realize he has a lot more fun up at the rim of these cesspools. Up here he has the opportunity to bump into new people. These people had every intention of staying clean. Unfortunately, they didn't see proximity to sin as dangerous ground. Maybe they identified the danger but were confident they had enough strength to handle it. Along came a roaring lion seeking someone to devour.

Honestly, this situation bugs me. Not so much because of the foolishness of people hanging out so close to the problems that will defeat them, but because of how often they aren't able to look back afterward and admit they enabled their own downfall. Far too many people bemoan the circumstances of their life without realizing they cooperated with the devil in creating those conditions. Proverbs 19:3 says, "A man's own foolishness leads him astray, yet his heart rages against the LORD." I think the modern way of putting it is, "Why is God doing this to me?" The Lord had less to do with it than the collaboration of our own behavior and the devil's schemes.

There are several specific ways to avoid dancing in the devil's playground. In order to stay away from the line of sin, we must bust every pattern associated with the sin. Getting out of the devil's playground isn't always easy, but we must stop frequenting the places, events, people, and patterns associated with sin.

For many people, the greatest challenge they face in life is maintaining healthy relationships. In regards to dancing in the devil's playground, there is no more common problem than the way we treat the opposite gender. People go to lunch with friends and coworkers with no concern for whether they are male or female. It's far wiser to limit our casual lunches to same-gender acquaintances. If this seems too extreme, then consider going out in groups and avoiding dining alone with members of the opposite sex.

If any suggestion to keep our hearts clean seems too extreme, then it reflects our love of the wrong things. I once knew a man whose wife fell into an affair with her boss. It started with the two of them going out to lunch, with the rest of the office, once a month. After a few months, the boss and this employee began hanging around afterward for short, but deep and personal, talks.

Here is my second suggestion for getting off the devil's playground in the arena of relationships. Don't share in emotional conversations with members of the opposite gender unless it's your spouse or your spouse is present.

The boss and employee both lost their families, their jobs, their reputations, and their self-respect when their sharing erupted into a passionate encounter. The affair continued until it made big news in a small town. Two prominent members of the community made for good gossip. When it came time to fess up, both stated they never intended for the affair to happen. They both stated it overtook them suddenly and without prior planning. While I doubt the betrayed family members will ever believe their stories, I do. I believe they never intended for it to happen; but their meals together, time alone together, and intimate conversations were the equivalent of dancing in the devil's playground. The devil was happy to give them a nudge.

Men are more susceptible to the devil's playground in some ways. Many men fantasize about the women in their life and feel like they haven't sinned, because they haven't engaged in any physical sexual activity. It's the old lie we can look but can't touch. It makes sense and has been the motto of many an unrepentant girl watcher. Most of the men I have spoken with see it as a bonus when a girl accidentally exposes herself. Maybe they look away in order not to get caught ogling. These men generally do not look away to protect themselves or to guard their hearts.

The lie that looking is okay doesn't end there. The viewer revisits those glimpses mentally and remembers fondly what they have seen. When our mind begins to find favorite people and favorite memories for these fantasies, we have an adult-sized crush. If we're already on the devil's playground for taking notice of the person, then we lean out over the edge of disaster when we treasure remembering those moments. These lingering thoughts are twice as dangerous.

These behaviors are mistakes. Matthew 5:28 says, "But I tell you, everyone who looks at a woman to lust for her has already committed adultery with her in his heart." It doesn't matter whether one is married or single. Don't believe the lie that says it's acceptable for single people to live out a different sexual morality than married couples. Sexual morality isn't only for the young, either. The moral standard for all of us is the biblical standard.

In fact, single people face greater dangers in these temptations than married people do. A single person more easily buys into the false idea, the fairytale notion, that a lover will meet all their needs and cause them to live happily ever after. Proverbs 14:10 says, "The heart knows its own bitterness, and no outsider shares in its joy." This verse is one of the hardest proverbs to understand. It teaches a tough reality; at some level, all of us are lonely. We long for a deep and unified relationship with another person. Things are complicated, because we romantically expect to find another person on earth to end this loneliness. When we get a glimpse of a potential relationship, we naturally read into it the hope that we've found the cure for our loneliness or unhappiness. The right person to share this with is God alone. We mess up our relationships and clutter our hearts trying to meet this need in human relationships.

Even our spouse can never totally comprehend our heart. Only in a relationship with God through Christ will we be able to fully share our heart with another. God understood everything about us before we were born. It takes a whole lot of work and maintenance before this relationship with God finds full bloom.

The natural man inside of us looks for relief from this loneliness in an earthly relationship. This natural hunger draws us closer and closer to the brink, even if we are strong. Not many people in today's society are strong, since most willingly jump over the edge. This difficulty is why, in 1 Corinthians 7:2, Paul encouraged anyone who struggles with their passions to marry.

It may help if we accept a difficult truth about relationships. They are an awful lot of work. The secret of a successful relationship is to accept the other person as they are while simultaneously working to improve ourselves and our service to them. Yes, you heard me correctly. The secret is to make it all about the other person. If this rubs us the wrong way, it's because we've bought into the false romantic ideal that our beloved will do everything to meet our needs and a relationship exists to be all about us. This is a selfish, romantic myth. Even when we are with the person whom God intends us to spend the rest of our life with, we will still be haunted by some of the loneliness mentioned in Proverbs 14:10. The relationship may not ease the loneliness, and it could make it worse. Remember, this loneliness was designed to draw us to God rather than draw us to our spouses.

Time and time again, I've seen a believer who was on track in every way until they fell into an unwise relationship and lost all their progress and spiritual growth. The worst case I've ever seen was when a husband from a neighboring church came to my office with someone else's wife from a different church. They were both planning on leaving their families and their churches. They came to see me to ask if they would be loved and accepted in my congregation. My patience reached the breaking point when they said, "But, God wants us to be happy." This statement assumes God condones their sin, because their happiness is more important to Him than their morality. We can never be happy when we know we are doing wrong. This couple was no longer dancing on the devil's playground; they fell right into the pit and refused to acknowledge they were drowning in the muck. They concluded by refusing to hear anyone who would not congratulate them on their impending death.

Where relationships are the first area of concern, addictive behaviors come in second. Earlier in this chapter we talked about people who justify alcohol use and how this activity invites destruction. Other addictive behaviors also need to be avoided.

The area I live in has a large number of casinos. Many people see no problem with gambling in moderation. Some start off in moderation and go on to lose their homes, families, retirement funds, and their self-respect. Even if we could guarantee we wouldn't be destroyed, why would we take the destruction of others we influence so lightly? If we see no problem with gambling in moderation, we are dancing in the devil's playground, and someone we care about will lose their life to this activity. In the spirit of staying away from the line of sin, I encourage us to stay away from casinos' other activities as well. Don't go to their buffets, shows, or other attractions. They often promote these activities to be great bargains, but it is no bargain if our heart is filled with the filth contained in that environment.

One more specific area of concern we must consider is language. Everyone I know has been embarrassed by an inappropriate word slipping out of their mouths. This happens not only because we encounter people using this language, but because we fail to notice when people around us use foul language. Some people I know will object when someone cusses around them, but most do not. Even the ones who object may watch television and movies where the same language is used. I encourage my church not to show movies. First, it's almost always a copyright infringement. This means showing it at church is illegal. But even if it were legal, we cannot trust other believers to tell us if a movie is clean or not. Often they say, "Yeah, I saw it. It was great. No language, sex, or anything." Then when we watch it, we find both.

This doesn't happen because we have a tougher standard than these other people but because they have gotten used to overlooking the language. When it goes by, they don't file an objection in their minds. Without an objection to make it stand out in their memories, they won't remember those words. The words are filed away in the heart and come out again at an inopportune time. We get off the devil's playground by preventing objectionable content when possible and filtering it when objections are not possible.

Sailors are not the section of society with the foulest mouths; it is high school and junior high school teens. Educational institutions no longer equip kids with the simple truth this type of language will hold them back in life. The strategy mentioned above is needed in this environment. Every time someone uses this type of language, object. Either object openly so the person speaking has a chance to change their pattern, or at least object internally so as to prevent the words from being unchallenged.

We must notice the flow in order to inhibit the flow. The best solution is to cut the channel of this communication by turning off the show or walking away from the person. Sometimes this isn't possible. If a teacher allows this language in a classroom, a student cannot walk away. If we mentally object every wrong expression, we hinder the corruption of it. If we don't correct this language, we'll adopt it.

Another concern about language is that objectionable expressions in previous generations are accepted as normal today. In the spirit of going big to honor God, I believe it would be wise to stay away from these terms as well. If our language is offensive, it's our responsibility to do something about it. This is true even if the phrase is accepted among our friends and found objectionable by people who aren't close to us. If we want to keep our heart pure, we must not knowingly offend others.

When I first started writing this book, my kids were both in their late teens. Every time they went to the store with me, they wanted to walk down the row with the ice cream in it. My kids loved ice cream. I hated it. I didn't hate it in the way I disliked consuming it. I hated ice cream in the way I really, really enjoyed it. I'm overweight. My solution to this problem was that I didn't wander down the row with the ice cream. I often avoided the rows with cookies, chips, and candy bars, too.

My kids asked me why I didn't buy ice cream more often. My standard answer was, "If I buy it, I will eat it." They said no problem, they would be happy to eat it for me. And, no doubt, they would eat some. Still, if I bought it for them, it always worked out I got more than they did. My solution became I'd almost never buy it. They'd still object, saying all I need is some self-control. I say I'm practicing self-control; I'm fully in control of myself when I choose not to buy it. This choice keeps me in control of myself later at home. The foolish notion we aren't practicing self-control until the ice cream is home and in the refrigerator is a variation of what we've been talking about in this chapter. I don't have to bring the ice cream home where it loudly calls my name. This would be choosing to step closer to the sin line. I would rather leave it in the store and not be nudged over the edge.

Chapter 14

DON'T STAY EMPTY

I enjoy going out to eat far more than I should, and I drink a lot of iced tea with my meals. Because of this, I prefer restaurants with free drink refills. Few things will cause me to limit the tip as not refilling my drink in a reasonable amount of time. There are many restaurants I intend to never return to, particularly places that don't refill an empty glass. It is amazing how empty a glass seems after a big, dry bite of food.

To keep our hearts clean, we need to learn to take full advantage of refills, especially free refills. I've talked about ways we must take things out of our life. By taking them out of our life, we prevent them from filling our heart with sin. Our life will be full of something. If we empty all the bad stuff out and leave our life empty, then we will be, well, empty. I encourage us to refill our life with better things that don't have the expensive side effect of polluting our hearts.

In Matthew 12:43-45, Jesus tells about a person who cleaned up their life and left it empty. Unfortunately, the demon that'd been thrown out returned and brought friends. The point of this story is that the house should not have been vacant when the demon returned. If the demon had found the life refilled, then it would have been forced to look elsewhere. When we pull things out of our life, always refill it with better things.

This emptiness is akin to living as close to the line of sin as possible. Just like the devil attempts to knock us over the line of sin, he also enjoys the opportunity to refill an empty life with the wrong things. The easiest way to make this impossible for him would be to fill the void before he gets the chance. Choose things God would want us to fill our lives with and things that fill our hearts in positive ways. These are like the free refills I mentioned earlier; they are refreshing and included at no additional price.

Christians use a collection of spiritual disciplines to fill their lives with good things. Entire books have been written on the topic of spiritual disciplines and are available to read. For this reason, I'm not going to go into much detail, but I will go over a quick survey of them.

The more spiritual disciplines we fill our life with, the less opportunity we leave for negative things to come into our storeroom and harm us. For this reason, I encourage us to go big in this area, too. It's wise to not look at these disciplines as doing more for God but as things we do for ourselves to keep our lives filled with good things.

I list these spiritual disciplines with no priority in the order I present them. I don't intend to make some of the disciplines more important than others. Nor do I intend to claim my list is complete. An individual may well enjoy a spiritual discipline I didn't choose to include. Every person is different and has their own preference based on how God has individually gifted and shaped them.

Let me begin by mentioning the Bible. God inspired this unique collection of writings to communicate to humanity His plan of salvation, His will for this world, His moral standards, and His nature in ways no other writing accurately captures. For this reason, reading the Bible every day is a great way to fill our life with something positive. In addition to reading it, we can go a step further and study a small section each day. Although memorization is under-practiced, we give ourselves immense advantages in life when we memorize passages of Scripture to guide us in daily choices.

When we use the Bible on a regular schedule, we notice several ways it impacts us compared to other reading material. We find particular passages jump out at us. We discover meanings in verses that haven't stood out at other times. These events happen because God is at work in us when we read His Word, interpreting it to us and causing us to grow through its teaching. The lesson reached out and grabbed our attention because He wanted us to understand it at this time in our life.

The second spiritual discipline is prayer. I believe a great deal more is accomplished in prayer than in physical labor, rational education, or any other human pursuit. We were made for a relationship with God. Simply put, prayer is talking with Him. Communication is the foundation of any relationship. Therefore, prayer is a central part of our relationship with God through Christ.

Prayer is not a single activity; it is a wide variety of activities that fall under this general heading. We should avoid using only one type of prayer in our relationship with Christ. We will consider prayer in four ways: praise, confession, supplication, and instruction.

One of the best uses of prayer is when we use it to tell God how much we appreciate Him. We do this by thanking Him for everything He has done or is doing for us and in us. We do this by worshipping Him and giving Him the glory only He deserves. Worship is also a part of praise when we describe our love for Him, when we tell Him how we feel about Him, His love, and His provision.

Another type of prayer is confession. This means admitting to God the places and times we've made mistakes. By bringing these instances to God's attention, we allow Him to forgive us and to cleanse us. This is what is discussed in 1 John 1:8-9. "If we say, 'We have no sin,' we are deceiving ourselves, and the truth is not in us. If we confess our sins, He is faithful and righteous to forgive us our sins and to cleanse us from all unrighteousness." The first sentence in the passage gives us the harsh reality. As a believer, we still make mistakes. If we don't deal with those mistakes, we fill our hearts with the wrong stuff. In the second half of the verse, the word cleanse means the harmful effect of the sin on our hearts is removed. We are not polluted anymore by the sins we confess. Therefore "fessing up" before God is a powerful tool for keeping our hearts healthy.

The most common way to pray is supplication. It is prayer for the purpose of communicating to God things that are important to us. Often, it's asking God to work in our lives in certain ways. Perhaps it's as simple as praying the teacher doesn't call on us to read in front of the class today. Or, it can be as complicated as asking God for a loved one to be miraculously healed of a terminal illness. Whatever the request, supplication asks God to work on our behalf. It is part of prayer, and everyone should be willing to voice their concerns to God. We shouldn't fall into the temptation of making this the only way we pray. We should always include the other aspects of prayer in our prayer life.

Also, remember that God always remains the boss and at times chooses a different answer to our requests than we expected or desired.

The last type of prayer is instruction. It allows God to direct our life through our time in prayer with Him. In other words, this is the part of prayer that allows two-way communication. Some people get uncomfortable the minute anyone mentions God speaking to individual people. Don't be one of them. Remember that the single greatest tool for reforming the heart is to let God give us a new one and to live according to the purposes He made us for. One of the greatest parts of living for Jesus is having a healthy relationship with Him. Healthy relationships must have communication between the two parties. At times, God wants to speak to us individually. This communication will probably come from internal leadings, not verbal communication. When we get good at hearing God's voice, they translate into very specific instructions.

Fasting is another spiritual discipline I encourage believers to try. Fasting is a period of time when we forego meeting our own appetites, while at the same time we seek God. A part of what makes fasting powerful is making ourselves more disciplined by keeping our appetites in check. Self-control always helps us to be better people, and this is a way of using self-control for God's glory. Another aspect of fasting is to use the time we'd usually spend on the appetite for prayer, Bible reading, and, in general, God time.

Fasting is usually practiced in terms of setting aside our appetite for food. In 1 Corinthians 7, it's clear it can also include other appetites, such as the marital sexual relationship. It seems to be a reasonable conclusion any appetite could be used as a fast. Nonetheless, the traditional fast is to forego food. I would encourage fasting not be over-employed and consideration be given on an individual basis as to whether fasting is harmful. I personally believe children, expectant moms, and people affected by different types of illnesses should not fast. Consider one's individual health and consult a doctor before pursuing a food fast. But, for the vast majority of us, fasting is a healthy activity we can employ to make our hearts healthy. If anyone does fast, be sure to do it with the intention for it to be a spiritual discipline. Redeem the time saved not preparing and eating food by making it extra time with God.

Another spiritual discipline is worship. It can include any activity that points to and glorifies God. Personal worship is a missing ingredient in many people's spiritual disciplines. People pray and study Scripture without including a time of worship. They miss out on a great opportunity. Worship can be somewhat ambiguous, so people tend to leave it out. It can take place in a wide variety of activities, and yet all of these activities can be done without it. A big part of what makes worship meaningful is the attitude of the participant. Sometimes a person undergoes actions they intended to be devotional, but no worship takes place.

Some of the common activities for worship include singing, praying, and preaching. It can also include a large number of others, such as dance, drama, meditation, and Bible study. In today's world, where technology opens so many new doors, worship can include video presentations, recorded music, and an unlimited number of active behaviors. All of these new possibilities can easily become nothing more than entertainment if we have the wrong attitude toward them.

When I encourage us to participate in worship, I believe it's important not to limit our worship to personal or congregational worship but to have both in our lives. Church membership is a commitment made by a group of believers. They agree to be mutually accountable in their Christianity and together they seek to carry out God's work on earth. Congregational worship is great, not just because it multiplies the glory being given to God by the number of believers present, but also because it is a group expression of this mutual commitment.

Church gives us an outlet for service. We need a place in our life where we can do meaningful things for God. This service to God is also a spiritual discipline. The specific activities may be mission trips to foreign lands or teaching children the Bible. We may work on a committee or in an elected position in service to the church. This service doesn't have to be glamorous or something others see, but we all need a chance to do things that make an eternal difference. We should be a part of the church God led us to. Just being present isn't enough. We must find a place in the church to work in a manner we clearly see is moving the kingdom of God forward.

Church also provides an opportunity for fellowship. This is having fun and developing friendships with other believers. There's a reason why we have so many potluck dinners at church. We like being with each other. This may not seem like much of a spiritual discipline, but it's a very important one. Time spent relaxing with other believers is one of the primary ways we rub off on each other. I can't count the number of times I've seen a new believer soaking in sound behavioral principles at a fellowship event, like an ice cream social. People who haven't learned the art of fellowship might be turned off by the words "ice cream social." However, when we spend time with people we genuinely like, it doesn't matter what we are doing. Good fellowship takes place due to the quality of the people, not the quality of the activity. The devil works overtime to convince us only morally degrading activities are truly fun, but he lies.

How does one develop spiritual disciplines? You can begin with the personal disciplines any day of the week. All you have to do is watch for a time in your routine to add a new activity. A sample of a morning routine might look like this: Your alarm goes off. You shower and get dressed. Then, eat breakfast and watch the morning weather. Fifteen minutes later, you get in the car and drive off to work.

The next step is to look for the opportunity. If I read my Bible before my shower, I will be back to sleep in no time. I'm better off picking it up after the shower or after breakfast. For other people, it might be a good idea to move beyond morning. Maybe they have a private office and a scheduled break. It might be better for this person if they use their break for some time with God.

After you spot the time you want to target, develop a simple plan. Many people fail in their quiet time attempts, because they bite off more than they can chew. If you try to commit to an extra hour every morning, then it will be easier for your day to crowd it out. If you find your window of time and start at a level you can maintain, then you can make conscious choices later to begin increasing the window. Remember to leave enough time to accomplish the goals of your time with God before moving on to your daily responsibilities. If your goal is fifteen minutes, set the alarm clock fifteen minutes earlier instead of cutting another activity down by fifteen minutes.

Begin the selected window of time with a short prayer. Now is not the time to be long-winded; just say hello to God, ask His guidance in the day's devotional, and move on to other things.

Next, I suggest a personal song. Private worship is a great part of this personal spiritual discipline, and it has a calming effect.

Once you've finished your song, go to a Scripture passage. Read one passage after another through a book of the Bible. It helps a great deal to not have to hunt for a passage. It's easier to use the passage after yesterday's passage. If you are getting started, use the Gospel of John. If you are a farther along, use some other New Testament book. Only after you've been successful in setting a pattern of personal study would I suggest jumping into the Old Testament. If you successfully set a pattern, you'll be ready in no time for the lessons of the Old Testament.

After reading a short passage of Scripture, pray again, asking God to use the passage to teach and grow you. Return to the passage again and look for a lesson God leads you to in this portion of the Bible. After a few minutes of studying the passage and giving God room to impress your heart with a lesson, you can conclude in prayer, this time giving God your current concerns.

After this time with God, you'll find yourself better prepared to tackle your day. When you've accomplished this fifteen minute goal for ninety days, you may choose to increase the length of the activity. Follow God's lead about how much time to add, and allow Him to guide the process. The routine might vary in the months and years to come. The direction will be as unique as your individual relationship with Christ.

We talked about the negative side of patterns and the importance of busting them. There is a positive side to patterns, and we can form positive habits to strengthen our hearts instead of tearing them down. Be forewarned, it always takes more time to build a positive pattern, a good habit, than it does to form a bad habit. Be ready to give it the time it deserves. Expect a little struggle with the details, but fight the battle to win. It will be worth it.

In addition to the personal disciplines, we need to form the basis for the corporate disciplines. This means looking for the right church to join. Although I recommend a Southern Baptist Church, watch for God's lead. Be sure the church teaches the Bible and salvation by grace through faith in Jesus Christ. Begin by attending worship. As you go through the worship service, you should pray and ask God to show you if this is the right church. Hopefully you'll get a confirmation either to join this church or look elsewhere. If you don't feel a confirmation right away, be patient, continue praying, and trust God to work in the process.

When you think you have the right church, double check to be sure you've covered all the bases. Have you spoken with the pastoral staff? This may prove to be very important. Do they have a Bible study you'll enjoy being a part of? Do they have services other than on Sunday mornings?

When you're certain you've found the church God led you to, make a membership commitment. If you are required to take a class, that's all the better. It lets you know what they expect. After joining, you should commit yourself to faithful attendance. For the best results, you should be involved more often than once a week. After all, you are maintaining the go big mentality. Anyone who feels God or a church asks too much of him says more about the condition of his own heart than about the church's expectations. Within a year, you should be in a solid habit of attending worship several times a week—prayer meetings, Bible study, and fellowship groups. You also should be serving the church in some capacity and growing in your ability to serve.

In the process of refilling your life with these positive spiritual activities, don't be surprised if the journey seems to be unusually difficult. The devil will be trying very hard to get you to back down and return to your old patterns. He wants to prevent you from becoming everything you can be in terms of accomplishment and usefulness to the kingdom of God. There are likely to be unexpected interruptions. Some people may claim to be offended by your activity. You might find unavoidable changes swallowing up the window in which you intended to do your devotions. These are the sorts of things the devil often uses to interrupt spiritual growth. Resist the devil, and he will have to retreat. Changing the patterns of your life is a great step in unleashing your potential. Go for the free refills. Refilling your life with positive activities—the spiritual disciplines—gives you a great advantage.

Chapter 15

Fordlandia's failure

In the early twentieth century, Henry Ford helped shape the world. His hugely successful mass production of the automobile redirected the way things were made in America Ultimately, it changed the world. What many people don't know about him is he required a high moral standard from the people who worked for him. He recognized bad moral behavior spilled over into bad work. When he assembled a team of people, he brought together people who were less-hindered by the slavery of sin. To put it another way, he brought together teams of strong-hearted workers. This is part of why his business prospered.

Henry Ford was involved in another project that was far from successful. He knew his plants depended on raw materials. If steel, copper wire, or rubber became unavailable, his factory would cease operations, and this occurrence would quickly get expensive. He carefully watched and guarded his supply lines. Rubber concerned him. The Far East produced all of the rubber in the world. The English and the Dutch controlled it. He was concerned regional issues such as social unrest or natural disasters could halt production of rubber and put him out of business.

His solution was to build his own rubber tree plantation.[1] He had agents search for a suitable tract of land and bought a huge section of the Brazilian jungle. They cleared the land and set it up to look like a small town in America. This location came to be called Fordlandia. Upper level workers at this facility consisted of workers who'd excelled at his automobile assembly plants. In fact, working at Fordlandia was seen as a reward.

Trees started from seed and eventually spread out across the plantation. A great deal of time, money, and sweat had gone into the project, and all seemed to be going well. When the time came for the plants to thrive and produce, they did neither. They became sickly, and nothing the workers tried made a difference. Fertilizers, watering systems, and insecticides were all useless. The workers were stumped on what to do next.

The problem at Fordlandia is a great illustration of the right people doing the wrong tasks. These automotive engineers were brought to a foreign place to do a foreign task. They were people with a great deal of heart, as proven in their previous success. People with great heart tend to have a lot of confidence and an adventurous spirit to boldly try anything. The problem was they were engineers, not plantation owners. They approached the problems in Fordlandia mathematically rather than botanically.

Eventually, they realized they needed to research the problem and brought in an expert who had the sad duty of telling them rubber trees could not succeed if planted too close together. In rubber tree plantations, the trees are kept far apart with native trees in between. If it isn't done this way, blight infects the plants. Further complicating the matter, the chosen section of jungle wasn't the best suited to such a project. The agents involved in acquiring the land didn't know what rubber trees needed and had been misled by the sellers. By the time they identified the problems, the project was unsalvageable.

These were great workers when involved in the production of automobiles. They simply were not the right team to build a rubber tree plantation. They didn't know rubber trees differed from plants they were familiar with in the United States. They boldly assumed if they put their mind to it, they could accomplish anything. However, an important and often obscure part of success is undertaking the right task.

A key question in the study of heart becomes, "How do I know the right task for me?" One answer is found in Proverbs 3:3. "Never let loyalty and faithfulness leave you. Tie them around your neck; write them on the tablet of your heart." This concept of the tablet of the heart is repeated in Proverbs 7:3. It is the manner God directs us in, both in terms of shaping our character and in terms of directing our path. The two verses refer to our choice of what we store in our heart. The tablet of our heart is also a practical way to let God guide our lives. Remember, whatever we store in our hearts will come out in our activities. Let God choose what to store there, and the output will be under His direction too.

It's the same idea as when we talk about "calling" in the New Testament. For example, Paul has a dream about a Macedonian man pleading with him in Acts 16:10.It says, "After he had seen the vision, we immediately made efforts to set out for Macedonia, concluding that God had called us to evangelize them." Paul and his companions understood this dream as God directing them. Paul filled his heart with a desire to see people saved, and this unction was used by God to call Paul to Macedonia.

Just as God called and directed Paul, He has a unique plan for our lives. He communicates His plan to us in some manner our individual personality will understand. The simple answer to accomplishing the most in life is to seek God's plan and to let His power assist us in accomplishing what He has called us to do.

How do we apply this to our lives? To begin with, we must have a clearer picture of calling. We have already said our calling is God communicating to us what He desires for us to be or do in a specific manner. This is commonly understood, but what is not always understood is that calling grows out of relationship. Our practice of the spiritual disciplines is our primary way of practicing our relationship with Christ. The only way to have clear instruction from God about what He wants us to do is to have the channel of communication open on a regular basis.

We cannot restrict the messages God sends so we hear only what we want to hear. If we believe we should be able to approach and seek God only on the topics of interest to us, then we miss the whole point of living in relationship. What kind of marriage would a husband have if he only came to his wife and communicated with her when he needed something? How much worse would it be if during those conversations he told his wife she wasn't allowed to bring up any additional topics but was restricted to only address his concerns? If anyone ever decides to try this, I suggest wearing a helmet! The better idea is to understand relationships involve free-flowing communication moving in both directions.

If we have made Him the Lord of our lives, we would certainly never limit His input to telling us what to do. In fact, God is more interested in who we are than what we do. It might be natural for us to want Him to give us direction, in terms of specific tasks to undertake. But, God is more interested in the process of making us into the person He wants us to be. Therefore, He is directly involved in shaping our character. I am convinced most of His calling in our lives is spent on issues of character. Why would God send us out to change the world if we refuse to change our own bad habits?

I taught both of my kids to drive. I followed a pattern to get the kids used to being in control of the vehicle. It started with running slow circles around a vacant parking lot. During this time, I had them follow my directions, including making sudden changes, such as braking hard or sudden turns. I might say, "Emergency stop; brake hard, come to a full stop!" At first they kept going and asked me questions like, "Why?" or, "You mean now?" At that point, they weren't ready for the traffic on the street.

Their reaction improved with time. When I said, "Emergency stop," I could see them think about what I said, then consider where the brake pedal was, and they would stop the car. It was funny to me how they consistently thought they stopped instantly, but as an observer, I could see a delay. They weren't aware of the time lost and would argue about it. What happened next was the exhilarating result of their trying to prove to me they could stomp the brake immediately.

Everyone I know, when first learning to drive, gets confused and stomps the gas pedal instead of the brake. This leads to some of the most memorable moments in teaching kids to drive. The car body still bears the marks of those moments. I didn't get very upset. I was just glad it happened in the empty parking lot, rather than on the road where other people would have been involved. At times like this, they still weren't ready for traffic, even though they felt they were.

Eventually, the kids got to the point where they didn't have to think when they needed to brake; their foot automatically found it, and within a tenth of a second we stopped. They understood the steering and never had to think which way to turn the wheel to control the car. Although it took longer, they came to the same understanding while backing the car up. Once all of these things were second nature to them, we were ready to take the car into traffic.

We can apply these lessons about learning to drive a car to learning to walk in relationship with Christ. Many people want God to lead them to a better job, to a great marriage, or in raising good kids. God wants to lead us to these things, too.

He also knows all of these things require adjustments to our character. He calls us to control our temper or our spending, or to develop self control. We believe God isn't communicating with us. This is not the case. He's telling us what we need instead of what we want to hear. For example, we may strain to hear where the next credit card payment is going to come from, while He whispers to us how to get through this month without charging more on the credit card.

Taking care of the little steps of obedience opens the door for God to lead us into bigger things. I have come to believe when a person turns away from a lesson God tried to teach them, God returns to the same point over and over again until they finally get it. Many people I know, including myself, seem to go back and relearn the same hard lessons multiple times. It's only after we get serious enough to make the changes in this current area of life that God can move on and deal with bigger issues.

In addition to allowing God to move us onto other lessons, every time we actually learn a lesson, we practice walking by faith. God leads us to adjust our behavior. We trust Him and try it. Our life is improved by these actions, and we see the benefit of having walked by faith. God gives a little tougher instruction, and if we trust Him again, we learn even better how to walk by faith. 2 Corinthians 5:7 says, "…for we walk by faith, not by sight." In context, this verse is a comment aside in the midst of a discussion of our heavenly reward. It makes the point that as believers we walk, or live, by faith. This walk of faith is a pattern or a habit that has to be nurtured and purposefully developed in our lives. The courage to trust God in big things is built by the experience of having found Him faithful in smaller things.

Living by faith means we are willing to do our best to hear and learn God's will and do it. Each step of faith is a risk. First, it is a risk because we have to trust that God will not lead us astray. For some people, it's a huge step of faith to believe God wants what is best for them. For others, this first risk is understood to be no risk at all.

The second risk is we might misunderstand God's will and do the wrong things. Unlike the first risk, this second risk has real danger to it. It is possible to misinterpret God's will. When we try taking that step of faith and find our attempt to follow God was correct, we get a little bit better at trusting God and walking in faithful relationship to Him.

Even when we fail to follow His lead, He is right there to teach us, cause us to grow, and shape our character through the event. In other words, God uses our failures to our benefit. Romans 8:28 says, "We know that all things work together for the good of those who love God: those who are called according to His purpose." The word "called" in the latter half is important. If God's work in us is His calling, then this verse promises even the hardest events of life are being used by God when we cooperate with Him. In this way, even our mistakes are His opportunities to shape our character and build our relationship with Him.

Here's a great hint about cooperating with God. Tell Him repeatedly that every minute of your day is His to use. Give Him constant permission to shape you and use you as He purposes. This permission tells God you want Him to work in and through you and urges Him to do so. It also takes the focus off of you living your life your way.

The prayer for God to be in control of your life is best done at frequent intervals. Little choices can be prayed about during the course of the day. Include permission for God to use the moment. When you feel led in a certain direction, God will be able to use the situation and you'll be able to let Him. If you find later you misread the circumstance, God will be faithful to use the event to grow you. God delights in taking a scenario the devil intended for discouragement or harm and thwarting him by using it for your benefit. Enjoy the irony of this; you can allow God to turn everything the devil throws at you to your good if you approach Him with the right attitude. Pretty soon it doesn't pay for the devil to continue attacking. Not that he will stop, but God will bless you in every attack.

In previous chapters, we learned filling our hearts with positive attributes flowed most naturally from our relationship with Christ. In this chapter, we learned following God's leading in our life, or His call, also flows from our relationship with Him. Following God's call on our life is the best way to open the doors of accomplishment.

I would not say significant accomplishments are impossible without this type of communication from God, but following God's lead gives us a serious leg up and takes the blind spots out of the process. The engineers at Fordlandia were caught unaware of some essential facts. This is part of the human condition, as it's never possible for us to know everything and take all risk out of our decisions. God is never caught unaware, and He is willing to guide us. The price for this type of insight is our ability to admit God is Lord of the universe, and it's only right to allow Him to direct our lives.

---

1 "Rubber Plantations," *The Henry Ford*, Copyright 2011, http://www.thehenryford.org/research/rubberPlantations.aspx

Chapter 16

The long road to integrity

Integrity is not a complicated issue. Both in the biblical use of the term and in the common dictionary definition, integrity means to consistently do the right thing. But, just because it's easy to define a term doesn't mean the practice of the concept is any easier. Integrity is difficult to live out, because it requires strict adherence and a long-term pattern.

If a person feels free to waver from right living, they are not practicing integrity. The unfortunate but common worldview in our society is that different situations call for different ethical responses. This way of living has undermined the integrity of our people and our nation as a whole. Once we accept immoral actions are justified by circumstances, we deteriorate into people who believe whatever seems to be pleasant or beneficial for us is morally right.

When we believe the line of sin shifts based on circumstances, we justify shifting it so we get whatever we want. I had a tough conversation with a woman who had stolen a large amount of money from the agency she worked for. She felt she'd been right to do so, because the group had a pattern of under-appreciating her. She believed the circumstances moved the line of sin. Such is the outcome of situational ethics.

If a person tries to maintain integrity in certain areas of life, but not in all areas, it cannot be integrity. By definition, integrity is holding to right behavior at all times. We have demonstrated in earlier chapters it is impossible to separate off areas of our lives. Desiring to have a secret area of life where we behave differently is a sinful desire. A person is not maintaining integrity if they permit such a desire to survive in their heart. A person who allows this desire to come to fruition is even further away from living with integrity. Consider James 1:13-15. "No one undergoing a trial should say, 'I am being tempted by God.' For God is not tempted by evil, and He Himself doesn't tempt anyone. But each person is tempted when he is drawn away and enticed by his own evil desires. Then after desire has conceived, it gives birth to sin, and when sin is fully grown, it gives birth to death."

If a person attempts to maintain right living but falls short on various occasions, they are not walking in integrity. It doesn't matter whether those mishaps are frequent or rare; every slipup is a breach of their integrity. "But, everyone makes mistakes!" This is true, but it doesn't change the fact integrity is a matter of strict adherence to a long-term pattern of right living. We may not like this definition of integrity, but it is the correct definition.

A number of years ago, a group of people I knew were talking about what it was like to be a born-again Christian. An unbelieving girl was present. She wanted to be included, and in order to break into the conversation she quipped, "I am a born-again virgin!" I almost congratulated her before I caught that she hadn't said what I expected to hear. The group laughed and graciously sought to redirect the conversation so she wouldn't feel left out. They also made two points to her. First, the salvation offered in Jesus Christ was something they took seriously. Secondly, some things in life have absolute consequences. There is no such thing as a person going back to being a virgin. There is also no such thing as a person having integrity while living by a pattern of falling into sin.

I want to be careful I don't define away all possibility of having integrity by equating it with perfection, but I'm also aware if I don't use a rigorous definition, we will all try to fit into a loophole in the wording.

I said all of this because I want it to be very clear there is no easy road to integrity. The idea that there are a few easy steps to becoming a person of integrity is oxymoronic. Integrity is not easy, and perhaps with a strict definition, it isn't even possible. But, it is perfection worth striving for. We will never meet a perfect standard. Only Christ ever did this, and human frailty in the face of sin will not change until Jesus comes back.

However, striving for perfection will always serve us better than finding some mark that is "good enough" and shooting for it. This mark we set will be conveniently lowered sooner or later.

As I have defined integrity, I purposely never included issues of reputation. Our true character is not always reflected in what other people think of us. I believe most people unconsciously try to shape other people's opinion of who they are. This can be as simple as dressing nicely, or it can be as complex as choosing which portions of a past event to discuss so the speaker appears to be more heroic. Other people's opinions are not the real issue of integrity.

This issue of caring what other people think of us is strong in the average person. When we claim we want to be a person of integrity we are often lying to ourselves and to others. What we really want is to be perceived as a person of integrity, rather than to go through the hard work and attention to detail needed in order to be one. We are prone to believe we are striving for integrity, when what we want is an easy way to enhance our reputation.

For this reason, we have to be careful not to trust what other people think of us or to decide this is what matters. One of the hard facts is very few friends will tell us if we are messing up. They may feel it would be discouraging or impolite. They may be afraid of losing our friendship. So, be careful not to use our friends' input as the sole measure for whether or not we consistently do the right things. I believe accountability is a great thing, but it is hard to keep in place for these reasons.

However, if we do happen to find a friend who will tell us when we mess up, keep this person close at hand. People who are willing to be honest with their friends are tremendously valuable. These are the people who can hold us accountable in regards to our integrity, as long as we are willing to allow them close enough to see our problems. Open and honest access is necessary for accountability to occur.

A number of men in my church have approached me in regards to pornography. It's a very, very common failure for men to view this material. I can often tell the difference between a man who truly wants to get past the problem and a man who only wants to leave the impression they are past the problem. I can tell which is which by how much access they give others into their lives. If they are willing to dispose of printed material, it doesn't mean much. If they are willing to dispose of printed materials and give their wife access to their computer logs, then we are beginning to get somewhere. If they do both of these things but refuse to let anyone near their office computer, all hope is lost. This is a person who only wants to appear cooperative.

I often use similar methods of checking up on families we assist with benevolence. If I bring in a food box or some other financial assistance, I will often go through their cabinets. Some people's reaction is, "See how little food we have left?" Other people react with paranoia. "What are you doing? That's my private stuff!" Once or twice while doing this, I found their private stuff, all right. I quickly found out what they really spend their food money on. It might be drug paraphernalia or large quantities of empty beer cans. People who have nothing to hide generally don't hide anything. People who have something to hide don't know how to be open and honest in any area of their life.

Often, I find people believe privacy is a great virtue. These people protect their privacy even when they have nothing to hide. I strongly encourage us not to be this way. I don't think we should tell every detail of our lives to every person we know, but I do believe we need to be open and totally honest with the people who are closest to us. This always includes our spouse, no matter how bad we think our marriage is. Hiding things from them is a bad idea and is likely to be the real reason the marriage is rocky. If we are lucky enough to find people other than our spouse who are willing to be totally open and honest with us, then make them accountability partners. This means we need to accept their input and be willing to give them honest input, too. It is only fair if the great benefits go both ways. Furthermore, we can only know how much effort the other person invests in us if we are responding in like manner.

If we have other people who are willing to help us out in this way, we have a great resource for honestly looking at ourselves. Our public reputation is useless for helping us see our own progress in moving toward integrity. An honest accountability partner will often be the clearest mirror we could imagine. This person will let us know where we slip up. They will also be able to discuss strategies for improvement. The best accountability partners never compare us with other people. If they see us performing better than everyone else they know, they will continue to focus on improvements we can make rather than letting us off the hook.

Being "good enough" is the enemy of real integrity. Comparing ourselves with others is totally missing the point.

Integrity, by the very nature of the word, is never the result of a quick fix. Technology continues to make everything faster, but the character issue God wants to bring out in each of us isn't impacted by technology. We don't like this, because we've gotten so accustomed to things happening fast. When it comes to becoming a person of integrity, quick changes usually won't be lasting changes. Despite our get-it-done-quick mentality, the most important things in life cannot be rushed.

When I talk with a person whose loved one has died, I emphasize grief is a long-term process. When I work with a couple who is either newly married or about to get married, I prepare them to expect the relationship to be a long-term process. Anyone who gives up in the first year of marriage misses the point. Resolving basic conflicts is what every marriage goes through at its start. After a couple of years, marriage begins to take on a different hue, and it takes a decade or more for the benefits of early work to come through. These are just a couple of ways character develops over the long haul. Integrity is a part of character and takes even longer than the above examples.

I see a lot of people who expect their failures should go away quickly and their right behavior should immediately cover it. There was the husband who claimed to go off to work everyday. He covered the fact he lost his job and attempted to make up for lost finances by frequenting casinos. When his wife found out, he felt as soon as he told the truth his integrity should be restored. He expected his wife to instantly trust him again. A lie that's continued for weeks will not be countered in days.

What about the mother who got involved in drugs? The father finds out, and they work hard together to break the addiction. The whole process takes five years from the start of the behavior to being clean and sober. After being clean for a couple of years, the wife restlessly wonders why the husband is still checking up on her. A short history of being free of the addiction doesn't change the history. The husband's concern is not a curse; it is his willingness to love over the long haul.

What about the teenagers who have been sexually active for months? There's a pregnancy scare, and in desperation they tell their parents. A couple of weeks later, they expect to be trusted out on dates again. Wise parents won't expect such an easy fix, and wise teens will understand integrity is not fully restored and is not easily patched.

The person who has sinned usually has their expectations backwards. They expect their bad behavior to have a small negative impact on their life. They expect their good behavior to have a huge positive effect. They expect their admission of guilt to have a large restorative effect. And finally, they expect retribution to be unnecessary to redeeming their character and reputation. All four of these expectations are dead wrong.

The first expectation is wrong patterns are not a big deal and don't affect the participant in big ways. Wrong activities undermine our integrity, dissolve trust with people around us, and cause us to have no self-respect. They fill our hearts with negative stores. The effects are neither small nor inconsequential.

Positive actions don't have as much of an effect on our hearts, character, and integrity. They are the normal behaviors expected of us. A person is seldom called a hero, given promotions, or admired for merely doing their job. Doing their job is expected. This doesn't mean if they stop doing their job this, too, will go without notice. In a similar way, humanity is expected to do the right thing. God expects it, and other people expect it. We improve ourselves every time we do the right things, but this improvement is not as big an issue as the damage done when we don't do the right things. It's always possible to work our way back from a failure, but don't be unrealistic and expect a short-term pattern of doing right to counteract a mistake, especially not a long-term pattern of mistakes.

The next false hope a person seeking restoration is likely to have is the expectation that once they confess their sin it will immediately be forgiven and forgotten. I'm not saying Christians shouldn't practice forgiveness toward one another. I would say we tend to act like children and hope saying we are sorry will completely put a transgression behind us. The reality is wrong behavior is wrong, because it harms people around us. This harm is not fixed by the words, "I'm sorry." Contrition doesn't make the situation better. It doesn't repair the internal damage to our hearts. Nor does it assist the other people we harmed in recovering.

Even in our relationship with the Lord, contrition for sin is incomplete when it stands alone. People seeking forgiveness for sin often get remorse confused with the biblical word repentance. Too many people believe repentance is being sorry for what they have done. Repentance is more than feeling sorry for what we have done; it's also turning away from what we've done and changing our patterns to doing the right things. In relation to building a life of integrity, it stands as a reminder. Contrition alone will not change our pattern.

In addition to being sorry for what happened and expressing the needed apologies, we need to try to set things right. People like to believe they are only harming themselves. I cannot think of a single situation where this is true. If we know we've blown it by doing something wrong, then we should be willing to look for how to make the situation better. This might mean paying for something we damaged. It also might mean paying for something we didn't damage. It might mean going the extra mile to ensure a person knows we care about them at a deeper level than making ourselves look good.

A few years back, a pastor friend of mine told me a story of his interactions with a church member. He was certain the member did not respect him or like him, but in the passing of time, they managed to work together. The member had a boat for sale, and after some pressure from his family, the pastor bought the craft. He took his family out on the water. That first day, an expensive part on the boat failed. They faced a large repair bill. When the church member heard about the breakdown, he sought out the pastor and paid for the new part and its installation.

The pastor realized he had a church member who could be trusted. They probably didn't agree on everything, but they didn't worry about each other, even when in conflict. They both knew the other could be trusted.

I wouldn't have thought it was the member's responsibility to replace the part. In my view, mechanical things break, and used things are always sold "as is." However, the church member made it clear his own rights were less important to him than the pastor's satisfaction.

It's a long road to integrity. We can live doing the right things for a decade or more, and it can all be undone in one careless act. Nor will any claim we make change our integrity one whit to the better. The road to integrity is only found by keeping our heart clean and doing so as a pattern for the long haul.

The rewards of integrity are great. A person who strives for this perfection will find a great reward already exists in the form of God shaping their character. If it's never recognized here on earth, the person who strived hard to maintain integrity will be recognized and rewarded by God in heaven. More than likely, it will be recognized here on earth; not only as the pattern of doing right, but also as the accomplishments of life it enabled. Keeping our integrity will fill our hearts with only the best of things, and those things will come back out in the form of great achievements on earth.

Chapter 17

GUARDING YOUR HEART

After the coaches comment at the football game, the verse the Holy Spirit ignited in my imagination to start me on this study was Proverbs 4:23. The entire passage reads:

> My son, pay attention to my words;
> listen closely to my sayings.
> Don't lose sight of them;
> keep them within your heart.
> For they are life to those who find them,
> and health to one's whole body.
> Guard your heart above all else,
> for it is the source of life.
> Don't let your mouth speak dishonestly,
> and don't let your lips talk deviously.
> Let your eyes look forward;
> fix your gaze straight ahead.
> Carefully consider the path for your feet,
> and all your ways will be established.
> Don't turn to the right or to the left;
> keep your feet away from evil. (Proverbs 4:20-27)

The first verse of this passage speaks of the importance of living wisely. Verse twenty-one reminds the reader how important it is to remember lessons learned. The third verse is an emphasis on these lessons being good for us, both spiritually and physically. Then there's verse twenty-three, which says guarding our heart is a top priority.

Before I elaborate on the verses in the latter half, I'd like to highlight verse twenty-one. I am of the theory there is a significant difference between hearing something and learning it. I believe as I've aged, my brains have been slowly leaking out. I don't mean to exaggerate the situation, but when I was a younger pastor, I could remember the names of visitors to the church for a week or two after their visit. If they attended the following week, I could easily recall their names. Now, I seldom remember the names of visitors, and as time goes on, I notice more and more often I forget the names of regular attendees.

I say this so those of us who are similarly stricken with forgetfulness will not feel so bad when I tell us the rest of what we need to hear. The truth is, remembering our spiritual lesson is critical to our progress. Years ago, I worked at a restaurant. After taking a few days off, I struggled to regain my normal working rhythm. The manager quipped I would never be allowed to take time off again, because he couldn't afford to keep retraining me. Although he was kidding with me at the time, his words struck a chord. I wanted to be a person who didn't have to relearn the same lessons over and over again.

I encourage us to be people who retain the lessons we learn. In terms of developing our character and integrity, if we do not consistently use the power of our heart, we'll lose it. If we don't continue to press forward, we slip backward. I mentioned the human tendency to decide at some point we've become "good enough" and stop moving forward. This attitude is a great danger, because when we stop moving forward, we unknowingly move in the other direction. We also become more vulnerable to satanic attack.

It's like taking early retirement, only spiritually, instead of vocationally. We no longer look for the next big accomplishment God wants to work through us. We stop watching for where God wants to grow our character. Instead, we sit back and make lame excuses about letting other people have a turn, being too old, or having reached our goals. The life lived with heart is not about our goals; it's about what God wants to do through us. If we're still here on earth, then He still has a purpose for us here on earth. When

He's ready to put us into His retirement program, He will also welcome us into His retirement home, an exceedingly large household with many, many rooms.

If you can't think of any other way to be of use in the Kingdom of God right now, then pray for the pastor. You'll be amazed one day before God how much you've accomplished in prayer. I have long suspected the infirmities of age were gifts from God designed to make us seek a strength higher than our own, a love that cannot be expressed in human strength, and a relationship deeper than earthly relationships. I have known senior saints who thought little of themselves and their usefulness to God, while their powerful prayer life shook apart the devil's schemes and solidified the ministry of their churches.

Early retirement is only one of the ways this danger of forgetting our lessons comes about. Another is not recalling the more basic lessons while moving on to the advanced lessons. I worked hard to have a Biblical Greek minor in college. At a time when school and life were pretty overwhelming to me, I conferenced with the professor. I wanted to know why I hadn't been able to grasp one aspect of the language. We worked the problem for a while until he noticed I messed up only when a certain letter of the Greek alphabet was used. The letter *xi* is formed when the future tense calls for a *sigma* to be placed before a *kappa* or a *chi*. Having moved well past the elementary foundations in my study of the Greek language, I lost track of one of the basic components. I have seldom been so embarrassed as to admit I did not remember a Greek letter *xi*. I could not write it, pronounce it, or grasp how it came to be used in conjugating Greek verbs.

There is a manner in which we can learn the basic lessons of heart, go on to more advanced lessons, and then realize the basic lessons have eroded out from underneath of us. Most people in ministry have experienced this. As they grew in Christ, they had solid prayer times, devotionals, Bible studies, and other disciplines. Then they began working in ministry, and, by necessity, they spent a lot more time with God and His Word. The problem lies in that the time was spent in sermon preparation and praying others forward. At first, this seemed like it would be a boon to their walk with Christ. But it often became a barrier, because there was a difference in time spent professionally and time spent relationally.

As quickly as I say this, I have to be careful, because I know some of the most worshipful moments of my life have been in sermon preparation. The two do not have to be mutually exclusive. But given time, the study we do because we have to be ready to lead others becomes different than the study we would do in order to love and appreciate God in our own life. In this manner, a person who studies the Word the most may become farther and farther from God. This problem explains the failures we see across the news from time to time.

In my work as a pastor, I occasionally bump into a person who wants to make a point out of the possibility they know the Bible better than I do. I would love to let every single one of them win this silly contest of theirs. Instead, I want to find out how well they know the Savior, not how well they know His written instruction. One of the lessons of heart is it is best applied in relationship to Christ. A simple knowledge of the Bible can serve as a stumbling block to the better gift, which is knowledge of God. Once a person is out of touch with God, the knowledge of His Word begins to take on a sinister selfishness. Devilish interpretations are no longer warded off by the Spirit if we no longer hear the Spirit's correction. I'm not saying we shouldn't study God's Word. I am saying knowledge of God's Word will not help us if we wander away from our foundational relationship with Christ.

Be careful as we mature and grow. At no point in the process should we decide it's time to take spiritual retirement or overlook the elementary principles. Remembering what we learn is vital. Only when we are careful with past lessons are we ready to move forward with more.

Let's return to Proverbs four, having understood verses twenty through twenty-two. Verse twenty-three is a transition in the flow of the passage. Up to this point, the words emphasize the lesson to come and how important it is. Verse twenty-three stands as a summary of the main lesson. It's like the topic sentence for this passage. Carefully controlling what comes in and out of our heart should be a top priority. Doing so will make our entire life better.

The verses that follow give five directions on how to guard our hearts. Those suggestions have to do with how we speak, think, desire, focus, and plan. A final word addresses whether or not we are willing to persevere in these tasks.

The first of these is mentioned in verse twenty-four where it says, "Don't let your mouth speak dishonestly." This seems like such an easy statement, but basic honesty is a foundational aspect of guarding our heart. Loosely spoken or thoughtless words are a constant danger to our heart. It is far easier for something to slip out and undermine our integrity than we'd like to admit. These words shape our hearts in the wrong ways. Verbal communication is our primary way of interacting with each other. Any discrepancy that shows up here reflects deep damage in our hearts and causes additional havoc.

The second half of verse twenty-four says, "…and don't let your lips talk deviously." The key word in this passage is deviously. The inclusion of this word in the phrase addresses more than the words we speak. It also addresses the decision we make prior to opening our mouths that we'll spin the facts in some manner. Deviousness is not just changing the facts. It could be choosing which facts to present. It may be arranging the circumstances in order to bring about a desired result. It's planning on a dishonest or manipulative level in order to control the reaction of others. It seems like this is pretty basic, but human nature can be manipulative without ever realizing what it's doing. This warning is about how we think in the course of daily life. We have to be diligent with ourselves, to think before we speak and to make sure our thinking isn't manipulating the facts.

The next phrase, at the beginning of verse twenty-five, says, "Let your eyes look forward." I believe this verse has to do with controlling our wants. I have mentioned several times we have to be careful what we choose to love. Great messes are made when we fail to control our desires. We must not allow ourselves to walk through life in wide-eyed wonderment seeking to have everything we see. If we are going to be one of the people who succeed, a big part of our success will be having the discipline to control our wandering eyes. If a person is serious about guarding their hearts, they keep their wants in submission to Christ. This is far from being apathetic or signing up to always go without. It's an act of trusting God, who knows what we need and will be faithful to keep His promise to provide it.

The latter half of verse twenty-five says to "fix your gaze straight ahead." This seems to be a parallel phrase with the previous, but I think the verse implies a little bit more. The word fix is important to understanding the passage. Fix means we need enough concentration to keep working in one uniform direction .If we constantly flip-flop our direction; we end up never getting anywhere. If we have to make a tough decision, we should take the time to write down our reasons why we decided as we did. This way, when the devil begins to attack the decision and tries to redirect us, we can look at the list and counteract the attack. Big decisions tend to have big consequences and require a lot of work. If the devil can move our focus off of the goal, then he has defeated us. Focus is another part of how we guard our hearts.

In verse twenty-six, it says, "Carefully consider the path for your feet, and all your ways will be established." This passage refers to being alert and watchful throughout our life. We have a tendency to want to live on autopilot. We want to deal with tomorrow as it comes. We all tend to fly by the seat of our pants from time to time. What this verse encourages us to do is get our life off of autopilot, pay careful attention to all the gauges, and carefully consider our flight plan. The simple act of thinking ahead is a great skill in achievement. By doing so, we may prevent all kinds of problems that would have occurred without this forethought. Think about our steps and the consequences of them. Plan carefully for meeting our goals, and develop contingencies for the little surprises that tend to come up along the way. If we take this extra step, we will make fewer mistakes and prevent some heart damage from occurring. Carefully plan our actions, and we will be guarding our hearts.

The final verse of the passage and the final verse of the chapter says, "Don't turn to the right or to the left; keep your feet away from evil." We have to not only do these five things; we have to persevere in doing them. We must decide to adopt these patterns as permanent changes. This will guard our hearts.

When our heart is kept from pollution, we protect our courage, our moral foundations, and our ability to accomplish great things for God. We must not overlook the importance of guarding our hearts in order to preserve our spiritual growth.

Chapter 18

A man after God's heart

In the course of this study, we learned to redefine the heart as a storeroom. From there we learned our hearts are strong or weak depending on whether we have been storing up good or bad things in them. Whatever we store in our hearts comes back out again in the form of future decisions and behaviors.

We took a closer look at different issues and concerns that commonly shape the hearts of people in our times. We discussed the importance of family as the first building block of the heart. After this starting point, we went over how relationships of all types have a special influence on the heart. Self-image, courage, and morality were reviewed as heart issues common in our society. From this portion of the study, we understood how dire the situation is for the person who wants to have a strong heart.

Then we turned our attention to strategies for having a strong heart. The single greatest thing we can do to strengthen our hearts is allow God to give us a heart transplant. We talked about the necessity of going big while breaking up the old patterns. This willingness to have our patterns completely changed is essential to being a person of heart. In order to accomplish this, we discussed two specific pieces of advice at length. First, staying out of the devils playground, and second, using free refills to fill our lives with good patterns. Staying out of the devil's playground meant not enjoying proximity to sin; physically, mentally or emotionally. The point of free refills was to avoid leaving empty spots in our lives that the devil could take advantage of. A steady practice of the spiritual disciplines fills the empty parts of our lives and doesn't leave room for the devil's input.

Finally, in recent chapters, we went over more advanced topics of heart. We looked at the concept of calling, in order to find achievement, by following God's lead. Recognizing our calling has two parts. God calls us to have a certain character and calls us to specific activities. We learned to acknowledge character must come first. But once we are willing to let Him shape who we are, He is able to use us in specific tasks of His choosing.

After this, we reminded ourselves there cannot be simple, quick steps to being a person of integrity. Integrity is a long and difficult journey to becoming the person God wants us to be. Concern over how other people see us is a distraction to real integrity.

Most recently, we looked again at the concept of guarding our heart, being sure the progress and lessons built therein are maintained.

Having discussed all of these things, I want to leave us with some final thoughts, the first of which is another biblical example. King David is repeatedly used as a standard by which other kings are compared. The first instance is in 1 Kings 9:4, where God addresses Solomon as he becomes king.

"As for you, if you walk before Me as your father David walked, with integrity of heart and uprightness, doing everything I have commanded you, and if you keep My statutes and ordinances, I will establish your royal throne over Israel forever, as I promised your father David: You will never fail to have a man on the throne of Israel."

In this phrasing, and in several other places, we see David uplifted as a great example of heart. This first passage describes him as a person "with integrity of heart and uprightness." In Acts 13:22, he is again described as a person of heart. The phrasing in Acts says he is "a man after My heart." In this phrasing, the antecedent for 'My' is God, and therefore David is designated as a man after God's heart.

Being a man after God's heart means David developed the heart God wanted him to have. It's a stretch for a human to imitate God in any way. However, we can choose to agree with God and trust Him. Doing so requires suppressing the selfishness inherent in humanity, but it can be done. Adopting God's ethics, courage, and purpose was what made David strong. It made him useful to God on earth.

David was a man God used in great ways, because he was a man who cared for what God cared for. Because he started with such great priorities and because God's call chose that time and that man, great things were accomplished in his life. I have reiterated several times we dare not assume God doesn't want to use us in mighty ways. I want to add that we live in times when God needs people who can be used in mighty ways. Our world is getting messier, and God is looking for men and women who are willing to point to the truth. Am I going to be one of them, and are you willing to be one of them? Do we desire to see the world around us redirected in a major way?

If these challenges awaken a stirring of desire inside of us, let's not back down. We must not convince ourselves we are too busy with our jobs, families, and lives to be available to God. We want to be people who rise to the opportunities God has for us. We must prepare ourselves by working hard to guard our hearts, develop our character, and seek God's call in our lives. Don't be surprised if God, in His sovereignty, chooses to use us right where we are. Accomplishing great things can happen in our current place, job, and family. The life we have right now may have already been prepared by God, Who awaits our decision and availability.

If we are willing to be used by God, there is no telling what He might accomplish through us. Perhaps what God would accomplish through us would be the next great accomplishment of humankind–finding a cure for some disease, inventing a life-changing device, unlocking a better source of energy, or awakening revival in our times. Maybe what God would accomplish through us would be the redirecting of public attitudes, which are currently shifting hard and fast toward hating God and everything He stands for. I can only imagine and dream about the great things God might do in us. I can't help but dream big, because I know God. God is big. God does big things in people who are committed to Him. God knows how to use a person whose heart is undivided.

Again, are we ready? I know the honest answer for most people reading these words is we are not ready. We are not the person of character yet. Therefore, we have some work to do before we are ready to be used by God in a big way. For the majority of readers, a slightly different question is appropriate. Are we willing to get ready? Are we going to give our entire life over to Christ? Are we going to love what He loves? Are we going to allow His call to shape our character? Remember, the goal is to become a new creation—not to look like a new creation, or to have our friends think of us as a new creation—but to actually and honestly be one.

If we are ready, then take a moment and pray it out with God. Give Him full control of your character and your direction. Give Him permission to remove every unclean thing within you. Even if it means He needs to shake you up in big, big ways, give Him permission to do so. We must voice to Him we love Him above ourselves, and we trust Him to remodel every aspect of who we are and what we do. After you make this decision, be patient, stay committed to it, and wait for God to work. He'll work on your character, and He'll use you in His kingdom.

I've listed character issues first, but we might be surprised how quickly God puts us to work once we're submitted to Him. I'm not saying it will happen fast, but it might. God isn't predictable in these matters. God has no reason to be predictable to humanity. Many times God will use a child, a new believer, or some other unlikely person to accomplish His will on earth. Therefore, it's important we don't look at what I've said and take it as an absolute. Don't believe you must have years of preparation before God uses you. You might have a time of preparation, and you might not. If you gave Him permission to move forward in His own way and timing, then you cannot build your expectations into the outcome.

But, one thing is predictable; God prefers to work with our cooperation. He prefers for us to want to be used. So step up. We have to make a choice. We can learn, remember, and apply the lessons of heart. If we do, we open up a door for our relationship with God to be played out in accomplishment on an eternal scale. If we fail to make this choice and live life as it comes, we won't see our relationship with Christ direct our future or who we become. We may be perfectly happy with our Christian commitment in comparison with other believers. This comparison is meaningless. Living this way, we will never know what might have been possible if we had been willing to surrender our hearts to God's will and call.

I heard Chuck Swindoll use an illustration on the radio. Abraham Lincoln went to a worship service and afterward was questioned by reporters. The reporters wanted to know what Lincoln thought of the sermon. He replied it was well-thought-out, presented eloquently, and made good points. The reporters said the president must have thought the preacher did a good job. The president shocked them by saying he thought the preacher had failed. When asked how so, the president said he had not asked anything great of the congregation.

Preachers often fail because we don't challenge believers to do anything great. We serve the One True God; He is a great God. We should be about the business of doing great things, or we should quit pretending we serve Him. I don't want to fail to challenge us to do something great. President Lincoln was aware he lived in a time that called for men to make great sacrifices, face great moral issues, and ultimately, pick the direction of the world for years to come. King David also impacted the world through the power of his heart.

We need to see our world redirected in similar ways. We live in an age that has forgotten the necessity of personal responsibility. We live in a time when moral shifts come quickly and disastrously one after another. If we fail to correct the course, we'll be setting a perilous tone that will last for many generations. We can rise up and make ourselves available to God, and perhaps He will use us to change the world.

I am convinced there have been times in the history of our nation the people understood the power of heart. I also am convinced that for several generations the lessons of heart have been deteriorating. Recently, while watching television, I heard a frightening statistic. When asked if they thought our nation would survive another one hundred years, 75 percent of the people said yes. This means one out of four people surveyed were not confident our nation would survive much longer. It amazes me anyone would think this way, but I probably shouldn't be surprised after studying heart for so long. After all, without heart, we don't have the power to defend ourselves.

My desire is to relearn the power of heart, in the church first and then in society as a whole. I want to see us become a people who understand the connection between right behavior and great accomplishment. I also want to see us become the people God uses to bring the Gospel to the entire world.

It all begins with personal responsibility and individual choices–mine and yours.

CPSIA information can be obtained at www.ICGtesting.com
Printed in the USA
BVOW011721230712

295960BV00006B/1/P

9 781462 719464